Partners in the Gospel

*An Examination of What the Bible Teaches about
the Roles of Men and Women in the Church*

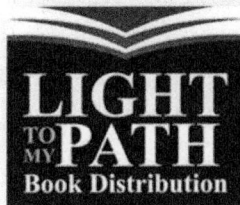

LIGHT
TO MY PATH
Book Distribution

F. Wayne Mac Leod

Light To My Path Book Distribution
Sydney Mines, NS, CANADA B1V 1Y5

Partners in the Gospel

Copyright © 2018 by F. Wayne Mac Leod

Table of Contents

INTRODUCTION

The role of women in the ministry of the church has been a hotly debated topic for many years. Many books have been written on the subject. The arguments for the role of women in the ministry of the church have been both Biblical and social in nature.

There are those who read the Biblical texts about women in ministry and interpret them literally for all cultures and times. Other people see the passages to apply to the culture of the time where women were not as educated and free as they are in our day. Then there are those who go as far as to say that the teaching of the Bible on this subject is outdated and no longer relevant to our present-day church. Let me tell you at the very outset of this study where I stand on this matter.

First, I believe that *the Bible speaks authoritatively to all cultures and times*. The Bible will not become outdated with time. What Jesus taught is applicable to us in our day as much as it was for the apostles who wrote it. God reveals His purpose for the church in His Word. He has given us His Word to be a guide in doctrine and practice until He returns. The principles taught in Scripture, apply to all cultures. How those principles are lived out may differ from culture to culture but all cultures in all times are expected to walk in the truth taught in the Word of God. It is our authority in all matters of doctrine and Christian life. If we are to understand the role of women in the ministry of the church, we must look to the teaching of Scripture as our standard and authority in what God requires.

Secondly, *God expects us to obey His Word whether we like what it teaches or not.* We cannot pick and choose what we want to obey. Let me be honest here. If you were to ask me what I felt about the place of women in ministry I could give you two answers.

On the one hand I could tell you my opinion, based on my personal experience and understanding. I could tell you about women who preach and teach as well as any man I have met. I could speak of the incredible impact of godly women on my life and faith. I could point you to examples of businesses and countries that have been led by capable and gifted women. I could tell you that men and women stand before God as equals. I could remind you of the wonderful gifts God has given to women that need to be used in the body of Christ.

On the other hand, I could take you directly to the Scripture. We could sit down and discuss the teaching of Paul and the example of Jesus. As we do so, I might find myself in a dilemma. Does what Paul teaches fit my personal opinion? Do I agree with him about the role of women in ministry? To be honest, there are times when I find that my opinion clashes with what the Scriptures teach. What am I to do when I don't like what I see in Scripture? After careful examination of the teaching of Scripture my obligation, as a follower of the Lord Jesus, is to surrender to it and accept God's way above my own.

Thirdly, we must realise that if we are to properly understand and apply the Scriptures we must take into consideration the culture of the day in which they were written.
There are commands and teachings in Scripture that only
apply to us in principle. We read, for example, in Leviticus
19:27 that the law of God forbade the trimming of the beard
and the sides of one's hair. Is it wrong for a man to trim his
beard? To go to this extreme is to misinterpret the Scriptures. These laws were written in the context of the pagan
religious practices of Old Testament times. They were intended to keep God's people from imitating the practices
of these pagan cultures and falling away from God. The
practice of trimming one's beard would not be a stumbling
block today as it was in the days of Moses. Nor would this
practice be required of us as New Testament believers in
our day.

In our examination of the teaching of Scripture on the issue
of the role of women in the ministry of the church, we need
to apply all three of the above- mentioned principles. We
need to take God's word at face value. It is not outdated.
We need to commit ourselves to obeying what we discover
in God's word, whether we like it or not. Finally, we need
to be careful not to misinterpret Scripture by ignoring the
cultural context in which it was written. With these principles as our guideline let us examine the teaching of Scripture on this difficult subject.

F. Wayne Mac Leod

CHAPTER 1 -

CREATION AND THE FALL

The world view of the apostles and New Testament believers was rooted in Judaism and it's understanding of God and creation. This is the cultural perspective from which we must begin. Genesis 1-3 recounts the story of the creation of man and woman and gives us some key details about God's purpose for them.

In Genesis 1 we read:

26 Then God said, "Let us make man in our image, after our likeness. And let them have dominion over the fish of the sea and over the birds of the heavens and over the livestock and over all the earth and over every creeping thing that creeps on the earth."
27 So God created man in his own image,
in the image of God he created him;
male and female he created them.
28 And God blessed them. And God said to them, "Be fruitful and multiply and fill the earth and subdue it and have dominion over the fish of the sea and over the birds of the heavens and over every living thing that moves on the earth." (Genesis 1)

This passage has several details we need to emphasize.

First, notice that God created "man" in his own image. The word "man" used in this verse is the Hebrew word "*adam*" which refers not just to a male but to human beings regardless of sex. This becomes clear in verse 27 when we read:

> *27 So God created man in his own image,*
> *in the image of God he created him;*
> *male and female he created them. (Genesis 1)*

Simply put, God created both a male and a female human being.

What is important for us to note is that the male and female were created in the image of God. This distinguished them from the animals. They were equal participants in this image. While they were biologically different, the man and the woman both reflected God's image. Having been created in the image of God, they were both to be treated with the respect and dignity that this implied. To treat either a man or a woman with a lack of dignity and respect was to insult the God who stamped His image on their lives.

Notice secondly from Genesis 1:26-28 that God gave both the man and the woman dominion over the earth:

> *26 Then God said, "Let us make man in our image, after*
> *our likeness. And let them have dominion over the fish of*
> *the sea and over the birds of the heavens and over the*
> *livestock and over all the earth and over every creeping*
> *thing that creeps on the earth." (Genesis 1)*

God created a male and a female in His image and said: "Let them have dominion." The use of the plural is significant. Dominion over the animals and the earth extended to both the man and the woman. In other words, both Adam and Eve were given the responsibility to care for and administer the affairs of the earth. They would work together as man and woman to care for the earth that God had given them.

Notice finally from Genesis 1:28 that one of the roles God gave to man and the woman was to multiply and fill the earth.

28 And God blessed them. And God said to them, "Be fruitful and multiply and fill the earth and subdue it, and have dominion over the fish of the sea and over the birds of the heavens and over every living thing that moves on the earth." (Genesis 1)

This first man and woman were to have children together and fill the earth with human beings. Understand that God could have made human beings in such a way that they did not need each other to have children, but He didn't. He created man and woman so that they were dependant on each other to fully obey the mandate of God. The man would not be able to bear a child. The woman, however, was created in such a way that she could carry a child and deliver it into this world. Her milk would feed and nourish that child until he or she was old enough to eat solid food. The male and the female would have distinct roles to play in this God-given mandate to multiply and fill the earth.

The difference between man and woman is seen not only in their biological difference but in how they were created. According to Genesis 2:7, man was created from the dust of the ground:

7 then the Lord God formed the man of dust from the ground and breathed into his nostrils the breath of life, and the man became a living creature. (Genesis 2)

The creation of woman, however, was quite different. She was created from Adam:

21 So the Lord God caused a deep sleep to fall upon the man, and while he slept took one of his ribs and closed up its place with flesh. 22 And the rib that the Lord God had taken from the man he made into a woman and brought her to the man. 23 Then the man said,

"This at last is bone of my bones
and flesh of my flesh;
she shall be called Woman,
because she was taken out of Man."

From Genesis 2:19 we understand that the Lord God created man, the animals and the birds from the ground:

19 Now out of the ground the Lord God had formed every beast of the field and every bird of the heavens and brought them to the man to see what he would call them. And whatever the man called every living creature, that was its name. (Genesis 2)

Woman, however, was not created from the ground but from man. Consider what is taking place in this context. Adam has been discovering all kinds of animals and birds in the garden. God, in fact, has asked Adam to give them names. These creatures were all created from the dust of the ground. If God had created woman from the dust of the ground and brought her to man, he would have seen her as any other creature. When God took her from Adam's side however, He was distinguishing woman from every other creature that Adam named. She was not like them. She was like Adam because she had come from him.

We are not told how Adam knew that she was formed from his rib, but it is quite clear that when he awoke he knew she had come from him and was like him and not like the animals around him. This act distinguished woman from the other creation. She was created for man as a partner to him.

There is another important detail we need to see from the account of the creation of man and woman. Adam was the first to be created. While the birth order of our children does not mean as much to us today, in the Old Testament Jewish context, this order of birth was very important. Listen to the Law of Moses in Numbers 18:

15 Everything that opens the womb of all flesh, whether man or beast, which they offer to the Lord, shall be yours. Nevertheless, the firstborn of man you shall redeem, and the firstborn of unclean animals you shall redeem. (Numbers 18)

Every firstborn that opened the womb belonged to the Lord and was given to the priest for His service. If the firstborn was an unclean animal the owner would pay a price to buy it back from the priest and keep it himself. If the firstborn was a male child, the parents would purchase him back from the Lord at a set rate and that child would live with them. While everything belongs to the Lord, the Lord claimed the firstborn of all families for Himself.

The other important detail we need to understand about the firstborn is that he would inherit a double portion of his father's estate. Consider the law of Moses as recorded in Deuteronomy 21:

15 "If a man has two wives, the one loved and the other unloved, and both the loved and the unloved have borne him children, and if the firstborn son belongs to the unloved, 16 then on the day when he assigns his possessions as an inheritance to his sons, he may not treat the son of the loved as the firstborn in preference to the son of the unloved, who is the firstborn, 17 but he shall acknowledge the firstborn, the son of the unloved, by giving him a double portion of all that he has, for he is the firstfruits of his strength. The right of the firstborn is his.
(Deuteronomy 21)

This double portion was not to be taken away from the firstborn. He was to be honoured because he was the firstborn and given this double portion of his father's estate.

We see from this that the firstborn, according to Old Testament Jewish culture occupied a very special place. As firstborn he would have a special inheritance and obligation before the father. This cultural understanding had an impact on the teaching of the apostles about the role of woman in ministry. Paul refers to this in 1Timothy 2:12,13 where he tells Timothy that the woman should learn quietly, for the man was created first. We will consider this passage later. For now, simply notice that this cultural understanding of the firstborn and his privileges is used by the apostles later to teach about the role of women in the ministry of the church.

As we move on now to Genesis 2:18 we read:

18 Then the Lord God said, "It is not good that the man should be alone; I will make him a helper fit for him."
(Genesis 2)

God created Eve to be a helper for Adam the firstborn. As the firstborn, Adam had a great responsibility to care for the earth the Lord had given. He could not do this alone. He needed the assistance of the woman to help him to fulfil his mandate as firstborn of creation. As a helper, the woman was not inferior. Though her role was to be a helper, she was equal to Adam in dignity before God for she too had been created in the image of God. Together as firstborn and helper they would have dominion over creation.

What we see in Genesis is that even before sin entered the world there are differences in roles and titles. Man and woman were both created in the image of God, but they were not created at the same time or in the same way. Adam was created first then Eve. Adam was created from the dust of the earth. Eve was created from Adam's bone. Adam is created as the firstborn. Eve was created as a helper. This was God's intention in a perfect world.

The world in which Adam and Eve lived did not remain perfect. This first couple would fall into sin. Genesis 3 recounts the story of how Satan deceived the woman and caused her to eat from a tree that God had forbidden. She not only ate the forbidden fruit herself but gave some of its fruit to her husband to eat as well. Listen to what God said to Adam after he ate the forbidden fruit:

17 And to Adam he said,
"Because you have listened to the voice of your wife
and have eaten of the tree
of which I commanded you,
'You shall not eat of it,'
cursed is the ground because of you;

in pain you shall eat of it all the days of your life (Genesis 3)

The Lord God cursed the ground, Adam was to cultivate because he listened to the voice of his wife. There are two points I want to make here.

First, we observe that God had an expectation of Adam as the first created and spiritual head of this small family unit. He had a spiritual obligation to care for and protect his family. Being a leader is a lonely position. It means making decisions that are sometimes unpopular. While good leaders hear the suggestions of those under them, they must make the final decision based on what they feel is in the best interests of their company, church or family. This will often go against the ideas suggested by others.

Second, Adam listened to the voice of his wife and ate the fruit, despite the command of God. The accusation of God in Genesis 3:17 shows us that God expected that Adam would act as the head of the family unit in the best spiritual interest of that family. He failed in his obligation as leader and spiritual head. He chose instead to surrender this decision joined his wife in sin.

Genesis 3:17 is not only important for what it shows us about the headship of Adam, but it is also used by Paul in 1 Timothy 2:14-15 to show the reason why a woman should not have authority over a man in the church. We will examine this later but for now the point is that this creation story is seen by the New Testament writers to be the basis for their understanding of the role of women in the ministry of the church.

We have seen God's rebuke of man in Genesis 3:17. Let's backup and listen to what God would say to the woman after eating the forbidden fruit.

16 To the woman he said,
"I will surely multiply your pain in childbearing;
in pain you shall bring forth children.
Your desire shall be contrary to your husband,
but he shall rule over you." (Genesis 3)

Because of her disobedience, the woman would give birth to her children in great pain. Take note of the phrase: "Your desire shall be contrary to your husband, but he shall rule over you." Consider what is taking place in this verse. God created woman to be a helper. With the entrance of sin, her help is now changed to "contrary desire." God created man as the firstborn head. With the entrance of sin, that headship is changed to "ruling over." The entrance of sin did not change God's roles for man and women, it did, however, change how they exercised those roles. He would exercise his headship as a sinful leader. She would stand beside him as a sinful helper. She would suffer the consequences of man's twisted understanding of his God-given role as the first born. He would experience the consequences of selfishness, pride and rebellion brought on by sin in the life of his helper.

For Consideration:

What Scriptural evidence do we have in the book of Genesis that both man and women were created in the image of God. What is the implication of both being created in God's image?

Genesis tells us that God gave dominion to both the man and the woman over the animals and the earth that He created. What is the implication of this for both the man and the woman?

God created man and woman different with a need for each other to fulfil His mandate. How do our differences as men and women complement each other in this task? Why do we need each other?

What is the significance that woman was not created from the dust of the ground but from man? How did this distinguish her from the animals God presented to man in those early days? What implication does this have for us today concerning chow we treat women?

Why is it significant that Adam was created first?

God created Eve as a helper? What was the implication of this in her relationship to Adam?

How did God's condemnation of Adam after the fall show us His expectation of him as a spiritual head?

How did sin impact the roles God gave to man and women in the Garden?

For Prayer:

Take a moment to thank the Lord that He created us male and female in His image. Ask Him to enable you to see that image and how both men and women reflect this image in different ways.

Ask God to help us as men and women to fulfil His creation mandate to care for this earth as managers of His resources. Ask Him how you can be more faithful in this.

Take a moment to thank the Lord that He created us male and female. Ask Him to help us to find a way to work harmoniously together according to His purpose.

Ask God to help us to fulfil our creation mandate despite the sin that affects us every day. Ask Him to forgive you for times you have not been faithful to His creation purpose for you as a man or woman.

CHAPTER 2 –

WORSHIP IN THE

OLD TESTAMENT

We learned from the account of creation in Genesis that the Lord created man and women in His image to have dominion over the earth. While both man and women were created in the image of God, they were created differently and with distinct roles. Let's take a moment in this chapter to examine how these differences worked themselves out in the worship of the Old Testament.

Women and Men Worshipping Together

In Exodus 14 after Israel was freed from slavery in Egypt, Pharaoh sent his army after them in the wilderness. God opened the waters of the Red Sea for His children to cross. When the Egyptians followed, the Lord caused its watery walls to collapse on them.

Safely on the other side, Moses led his people in a song of thanksgiving and praise:

*1 Then Moses and the people of Israel sang this song to
the Lord, saying,
"I will sing to the Lord, for he has triumphed gloriously;
the horse and his rider he has thrown into the sea.
2 The Lord is my strength and my song,
and he has become my salvation;
this is my God, and I will praise him,
my father's God, and I will exalt him.
3 The Lord is a man of war;
the Lord is his name. (Exodus 15)*

After Moses led the people in this song of thanksgiving,
Miriam took a tambourine in her hand and led the women
in a celebration dance.

*20 Then Miriam the prophetess, the sister of Aaron, took
a tambourine in her hand, and all the women went out after her with tambourines and dancing. 21 And Miriam
sang to them:*

*"Sing to the Lord, for he has triumphed gloriously;
the horse and his rider he has thrown into the sea." (Exodus 15)*

This dance was part of the worship offered to God after He
delivered Israel from the Egyptian army. Miriam and the
woman played a significant role in this celebration.

We see a similar incident in 1 Samuel 18:6,7. David had
just come home from defeating the Philistines. As he entered the city of Jerusalem, the women came out to great
him. They sang and danced to celebrate the goodness of
God in giving them deliverance from their enemies.

*6 As they were coming home, when David returned from
striking down the Philistine, the women came out of all*

the cities of Israel, singing and dancing, to meet King
Saul, with tambourines, with songs of joy, and with musi-
cal instruments. 7 And the women sang to one another
as they celebrated,
"Saul has struck down his thousands,
and David his ten thousands." (1 Samuel 18)

We learn from 2 Chronicles 35.25 that both men and
women sang sons of laments in the worship of the Lord
God.

25 Jeremiah also uttered a lament for Josiah; and all the
singing men and singing women have spoken of Josiah
in their laments to this day... (2 Chronicles 35)

Among the group who returned to Jerusalem in the days
of Ezra were 200 men and women singers (see Ezra 2:65).
We also see in Judges 5:1 how, after defeating King Jabin,
Deborah the prophetess and Barak the military commander sang a song of thanksgiving to the Lord.

The women of the Old Testament were free to worship
alongside men. They sang and danced in celebration of
God and His great victories.

Men and Women Joining Together Under the Preaching
and Reading of the Word

Not only did women join men in the praise and worship of
God in the Old Testament, they also joined them in listen-
ing to the reading and proclamation of the Word of God. In
Deuteronomy 31.12-13 Moses commanded the assembly
of men, women and little ones to hear the reading of the
Law of God:

12 Assemble the people, men, women, and little ones, and the sojourner within your towns, that they may hear and learn to fear the Lord your God, and be careful to do all the words of this law, 13 and that their children, who have not known it, may hear and learn to fear the Lord your God, as long as you live in the land that you are going over the Jordan to possess. (Deuteronomy 31)

It was the purpose of God that men, women and children learn through the reading of the Word, how to follow Him and His purpose.

After Israel's defeat at Ai in Joshua 8, Joshua assembled the people to renew their covenant with the Lord their God. He read to them the words of the law. Men and women were gathered together to hear the words of this law:

34 And afterward he read all the words of the law, the blessing and the curse, according to all that is written in the Book of the Law. 35 There was not a word of all that Moses commanded that Joshua did not read before all the assembly of Israel, and the women, and the little ones, and the sojourners who lived among them. (Joshua 8)

Ezra the priest, as well, had men and women assembled before him to listen to the words of the Book of the Law:

1 And all the people gathered as one man into the square before the Water Gate. And they told Ezra the scribe to bring the Book of the Law of Moses that the Lord had commanded Israel. 2 So Ezra the priest brought the Law before the assembly, both men and women and all who could understand what they heard, on the first day of the seventh month. 3 And he read from it facing the square before the Water Gate from early morning until midday, in the presence of the men and the women and those who could understand. And the ears of all the people were attentive to the Book of the Law. (Nehemiah 8)

Nehemiah 8 goes on to tell us that as the words of the law were being read, the Levites instructed the people in the meaning of these words. The context clearly indicates that men and women were in the assembly that day. Women assembled with men under the reading and preaching of the Word of God.

Women and Men Publicly Confessing Sin

There are at least two occasions in the Old Testament where women and men are involved in public confession and weeping for sin. In the passage we have just quoted from Nehemiah 8, we understand that both men and women gathered to hear the Word of the Lord. Notice the response of "all the people" to the preaching and teaching of God's Word on that day:

9 And Nehemiah, who was the governor, and Ezra the priest and scribe, and the Levites who taught the people said to all the people, "This day is holy to the Lord your God; do not mourn or weep." For all the people wept as they heard the words of the Law. (Nehemiah 8)

"All the people" wept as they heard the words of the Law. These individuals, men and women, were touched by the truth of the word. Together men and women grieved for their sin against God.

Ezra 10.1 makes this even clearer:

1 While Ezra prayed and made confession, weeping and casting himself down before the house of God, a very great assembly of men, women, and children, gathered to him out of Israel, for the people wept bitterly. (Ezra 10)

Both men and women were being touched by the Spirit of God. Together they confessed their sin and grieved before God.

Women and Men Bringing Offerings to the Lord

Women, like men were encouraged to bring their offerings to the Lord.

20 Then all the congregation of the people of Israel departed from the presence of Moses. 21 And they came, everyone whose heart stirred him, and everyone whose spirit moved him, and brought the Lord's contribution to be used for the tent of meeting, and for all its service, and for the holy garments. 22 So they came, both men and women. All who were of a willing heart brought brooches and earrings and signet rings and armlets, all sorts of gold objects, every man dedicating an offering of gold to the Lord (Exodus 35)

29 All the men and women, the people of Israel, whose heart moved them to bring anything for the work that the Lord had commanded by Moses to be done brought it as a freewill offering to the Lord. (Exodus 35)

The Lord made no distinction between the offering brought by a man and the offering brought by a woman. All whose hearts moved them were free to bring their offerings to the Lord.

Men and Women Making Vows to the Lord

In Numbers 6.1-4 we read that both men and women were able to make special vows of separation to the Lord as a Nazirite.

2 "Speak to the people of Israel and say to them, When either a man or a woman makes a special vow, the vow of a Nazirite, to separate himself to the Lord, 3 he shall separate himself from wine and strong drink. He shall drink no vinegar made from wine or strong drink and shall not drink any juice of grapes or eat grapes, fresh or dried. 4 All the days of his separation he shall eat nothing that is produced by the grapevine, not even the seeds or the skins. (Numbers 6)

The Nazirite vow was a special vow of separation to the Lord for a period of time and for a particular purpose. It is quite clear from Numbers 6:2 that this was a vow of separation that either a man or a woman could take. There was no distinction made for this vow.

While women could make vows to the Lord, we read in Numbers 30 that there were some restrictions for women in the making of vows. The Law of Moses stated that the vow of a woman who still lived at home with her parents could be annulled by her father if he disapproved:

3 "If a woman vows a vow to the Lord and binds herself by a pledge, while within her father's house in her youth, 4 and her father hears of her vow and of her pledge by which she has bound herself and says nothing to her, then all her vows shall stand, and every pledge by which she has bound herself shall stand. 5 But if her father opposes her on the day that he hears of it, no vow of hers,

*no pledge by which she has bound herself shall stand.
And the Lord will forgive her, because her father opposed
her. (Numbers 30)*

The same principle applied to a woman who had a husband. If the husband, as the head of the household, disapproved of the vow his wife made, he could annul the vow:

*6 "If she marries a husband, while under her vows or any
thoughtless utterance of her lips by which she has bound
herself, 7 and her husband hears of it and says nothing to
her on the day that he hears, then her vows shall stand,
and her pledges by which she has bound herself shall
stand. 8 But if, on the day that her husband comes to
hear of it, he opposes her, then he makes void her vow
that was on her, and the thoughtless utterance of her lips
by which she bound herself. And the Lord will forgive her.
(Numbers 30)*

In the matter of making vows to the Lord, while the woman was free to do so, she would need to have the approval of the head of her household, whether she be an unmarried woman or a married woman.

Exhorting Men in Spiritual Matters

On several occasions in Scripture, women were used by the Lord to exhort men who failed in their responsibilities before God. In Exodus 4.24-26 we read how the Lord sought to put Moses to death. His wife Zipporah, however, took a flint knife and cut off the foreskin of their youngest son, appeasing the wrath of God and saving her husband's life. Moses had failed in his responsibilities as spiritual head of the family by not circumcising their son. His wife rebuked him by saying: "Surely, you are a bridegroom of blood to me" (Exodus 4:25). Were it not for her actions, Moses may never have reached Egypt. When Moses failed in his obligation, she took on his role and spared the family. While this responsibility belonged to the male head of the family, in this case, Zipporah, as the wife took it on because of her husband's failure to be the leader he needed to be.

Deborah exhorted Barak to take courage and fight their enemy Sisera and his forces. It appears that Barak was fearful of taking on this responsibility. Deborah, however, challenged him to be faithful to the direction of the Lord and the responsibilities he had as a military commander.

6 She sent and summoned Barak the son of Abinoam from Kedesh-naphtali and said to him, "Has not the Lord, the God of Israel, commanded you, 'Go, gather your men at Mount Tabor, taking 10,000 from the people of Naphtali and the people of Zebulun. (Judges 4)

Barak would only agree to go to war against Sisera if Deborah went with him.

8 Barak said to her, "If you will go with me, I will go, but if you will not go with me, I will not go." 9 And she said, "I will surely go with you. Nevertheless, the road on which you are going will not lead to your glory, for the Lord will sell Sisera into the hand of a woman." Then Deborah arose and went with Barak to Kedesh. (Judges 4)

Because he did not trust the Lord and take this responsibility willingly, Barak would not be the one to defeat Sisera. Instead, Jael, the wife of Heber would kill this great military commander when he came to her tent for refreshment and rest (see Judges 4:17-22). Were it not for the exhortation of Deborah, Sisera might have ravaged the land. She needed to challenge Barak to be the leader God had called him to be. These women had a vital role to play in challenging the man of their nation and families to be the leaders God had called them to be.

Women Ministering at the Tabernacle

Women also had a ministry in the tabernacle. We have references to their ministry at the entrance of this tent of meeting. We read, for example of how Bezalel made the basin used for the tabernacle out of the mirrors of the women who ministered in the entrance of the tent of meeting:

8 He made the basin of bronze and its stand of bronze, from the mirrors of the ministering women who ministered in the entrance of the tent of meeting. (Exodus 38)

Eli, the priest had sons who served as priests. The Scriptures describe them as worthless men who did not know the Lord (1 Samuel 2:12). One of their abominable sins is described in 1 Samuel 2:22:

22 Now Eli was very old, and he kept hearing all that his sons were doing to all Israel, and how they lay with the women who were serving at the entrance to the tent of meeting. (1 Samuel 2)

Eli's sons slept with the women who were serving at the entrance of the tent of meeting. Obviously, these women were not present at the entrance of the tabernacle for prostitution, otherwise they would have been quickly removed for this was clearly against the Law of Moses. Exodus 38:8 describes what they were doing as "ministry." 1 Samuel 2:12 defines it as "service."

While we are not certain as to the exact nature of the ministry these women had at the tabernacle entrance, it is assumed that they had a role of serving in clean-up or in being door keepers. Some commentators see the possibility that they were involved in singing and dancing for the special festivals celebrated throughout the year. Whatever their function was, it was in important part of the overall ministry of the tabernacle.

Beyond their function at the entrance of the tabernacle, women played other service roles in the religious life of the Old Testament. In Exodus 35.25,26 we read about the women who spun goat hair to make material necessary for the construction of the tabernacle.

25 And every skilful woman spun with her hands, and they all brought what they had spun in blue and purple and scarlet yarns and fine twined linen. 26 All the women whose hearts stirred them to use their skill spun the goats' hair. (Exodus 35)

These women are described in Exodus 35:25 as "skilful women". Notice, however, that this was a voluntary act on the part of these women. Verse 26 tells us that it was those whose hearts stirred them to use their skill, that made this significant contribution. They are recognized for their skill, tender heart, and generosity.

Women of the Old Testament also played a significant role in the ministry of hospitality. The Lord commanded a widow in Zarephath to provide for the needs of His servant Elijah.

8 Then the word of the Lord came to him, 9 "Arise, go to Zarephath, which belongs to Sidon, and dwell there.

Behold, I have commanded a widow there to feed you."
(1 Kings 17)

God called this widow to support the prophet and provided him with a home. This would have been a tremendous blessing for Elijah in his time of need.

Elijah's successor, Elisha, experienced the same kind of blessing when he ministered in the region of Shunem. Listen to the account of what happened in 2 Kings 4:

8 One day Elisha went on to Shunem, where a wealthy woman lived, who urged him to eat some food. So whenever he passed that way, he would turn in there to eat food. 9 And she said to her husband, "Behold now, I know that this is a holy man of God who is continually passing our way. 10 Let us make a small room on the roof with walls and put there for him a bed, a table, a chair, and a lamp, so that whenever he comes to us, he can go in there." (2 Kings 4)

Not only did this wealthy woman generously provide food for Elisha but she spoke to her husband about making a small room on their roof with a bed, table, chair and lamp where Elisha could stay every time he passed through the region. She used her wealth to offer hospitality to the servant of God. We get a glimpse of how grateful the prophet was in 2 Kings 4:13-17 when he asked her what he could do in return for her great generosity. The woman had never had a child but when Elisha committed this matter to the Lord, she and her husband were blessed with an heir.

In 1 Samuel 1:9-11 we meet the mother of Samuel the prophet, at the temple where she had come to pray for a son and make a vow to dedicated him to the Lord. She would return the following year to offer this son Samuel to full-time service for the Lord (1 Samuel 1:26-28). She could not have made a greater sacrifice. Her son, would become one of the greatest prophets the nation of Israel knew.

These women were faithful servants of God. They devoted themselves to using their skills and resources for the Lord. Their time, effort and generosity were blessed by the Lord for the expansion of His kingdom.

Women receiving Words from God

Samson' s mother received a visit from an angel in Judges 13. This angel told her that she would give birth to a son who would deliver Israel from their bondage.

Miriam, the sister of Moses is described in Exodus 15:20-21 as a prophetess. She took her tambourine and led the women of the day in dancing and singing worship and praise to the Lord who had delivered them from the Egyptians.

Listen to the ministry of Deborah the prophetess as described for us in Judges 4:

4 Now Deborah, a prophetess, the wife of Lappidoth, was judging Israel at that time. 5 She used to sit under the palm of Deborah between Ramah and Bethel in the hill country of Ephraim, and the people of Israel came up to her for judgment. (Judges 4)

Notice the phrase, "the people of Israel came up to her for judgment." The idea here is that these individuals needed to resolve their problems and wanted to know what the

Lord's direction was for them. They would come to Deborah and she would consult the Lord on their behalf.

After discovering the Book of the Law in the long-forsaken temple, King Josiah commanded the priest Hilkiah to inquire of the Lord for him (2 Kings 22:12,13). The priest and his servants found Huldah the prophetess and consulted her. She sought the word of the Lord for these men and they returned with this word to the king (see 2 Kings 22:14-20). Through Huldah, the Lord would remind these men of the judgement to come.

God spoke through prophetesses to the male leadership of their day challenging them to turn to God. The prophetic gift was not limited to men. Nor was a woman with this gift limited to using her gift for women alone.

Women Deliverers

The Bible recounts the stories of numerous women who brought deliverance to Israel from her enemies. Were it not for Deborah, Barak would not have defeated the army of Sisera (see Judges 4). Jael killed the military commander Sisera, relieving Israel from this cruel oppressor (see Judges 4.18-23). Abimelech, the evil king, was killed by a woman who threw a stone on his head from the city wall of Thebez (see Judges 9:50-55). Abigail's wise advice kept David from wiping out the entire family of Nabal (see 1 Samuel 25). These women were used of God bring great victory to the people of God in times of crisis.

RESTRICTIONS

From what we have seen women were very active in the religious life of Israel. There were, however, certain restrictions place on them. These restrictions fall under two main headings.

Uncleanness

The first set of restrictions placed on women in the Old Testament related to ceremonial uncleanness. To be fair, this restriction was also for men.

There were many ways a man or woman could become unclean. Touching the body of a dead person, for example, would make a person unclean before the Lord and as such they would not be permitted to bring their offering to the Lord (see Leviticus 9:6). If an individual was diagnosed with a skin disease, they could be proclaimed impure by the priest and forbidden to go to the tabernacle or even circulate among the people of God (see Leviticus 13). Another means of becoming unclean was by touching an unclean animal or insect (see Leviticus 11:13-40). These instances could keep an individual from worshipping the Lord until they were purified.

Beyond the above examples were cases of bodily emissions. For example, if a man had a bodily discharge he was considered impure. This discharge might be a discharge of mucus or pus from a wound and likely related to an infection of some kind in his body. This man was unclean. Anything he sat on would be unclean and anyone who touched him would be unclean (see Leviticus 15:2-13). This principle would also be true for a woman.

An emission of semen would also make a man unclean. If this was the result of a sexual relationship with a woman both the man and the woman were unclean and would have to bathe in water and wait until the evening until they were pure again (see Leviticus 15:16-18).

A woman was considered unclean for seven days during her monthly period. Anyone touching her during that time or anything she sat or laid on would become unclean as well (see Leviticus 15:19-30).

When a woman gave birth to a child, the Law of Moses declared unclean while she recovered. If the child was a male child, she would be unclean for 40 days. If the child born to her was a female, the mother would be unclean for 80 days (see Leviticus 12:1-8). It is clear from Leviticus 12:4 that during this time of impurity the woman was not permitted to go near the sanctuary of God:

4 Then she shall continue for thirty-three days in the blood of her purifying. She shall not touch anything holy, nor come into the sanctuary, until the days of her purifying are completed. (Leviticus 12)

These times of purification limited how often the woman could serve at the tabernacle or bring an offering to the Lord. The Lord required that those who worshipped Him (male or female) be ceremonially clean. Anyone who refused to adhere to these standards was to be cut off from the assembly of God's people:

20 "If the man who is unclean does not cleanse himself, that person shall be cut off from the midst of the assembly, since he has defiled the sanctuary of the Lord. Because the water for impurity has not been thrown on him, he is unclean. (Numbers 19)

Submission

We saw in the first chapter that God created Adam to be the firstborn and spiritual head. The woman was created to be a helper. The law of the Old Testament protected this relationship.

While a woman was free to make a vow to the Lord, that vow could be over ruled by a male head in her life. If she was still living with her father, her father had the right to overrule her vow. If she was married and her husband did not approve of her vow, he too could overrule it and it would no longer be binding upon her (see Leviticus 30.3-16). This reaffirms the headship of the male in the family unit and his responsibility to protect those for whom he was responsible.

In the Old Testament, the spiritual welfare of Israel was overseen by the priests and Levites. By command of God, Aaron and his sons were chosen to be priests (see Exodus 29:1-9). The Lord also chose the male descendants of Levi to assist the priests in their regular duties (see Numbers 3:5-39). Women were not given this role but were, like the rest of the people of Israel, to submit to the spiritual leadership God had ordained for the nation.

What was true of the spiritual life of Israel is also seen in the family life of the nation as well. The man was considered the head of the family unit.

4 And there shall be with you a man from each tribe, each man being the head of the house of his fathers.
(Numbers 1)

3 So Moses sent them from the wilderness of Paran, according to the command of the Lord, all of them men who were heads of the people of Israel. (Numbers 13)

The wife was seen in the Old Testament to be under the authority of her husband:

20 But if you have gone astray, though you are under your husband's authority, and if you have defiled yourself, and some man other than your husband has lain with you, 21 then' (let the priest make the woman take the oath of the curse, and say to the woman) 'the Lord make you a curse and an oath among your people, when the Lord makes your thigh fall away and your body swell... 29 This is the law in cases of jealousy, when a wife, though under her husband's authority, goes astray and defiles herself. (Numbers 5)

The law of Moses protected the headship of the man in the spiritual leadership of the nation of Israel and in the family unit. All who were under this headship were to be submissive and respectful of this leadership, whether they be male or female.

Women were quite active in the religious life of Israel. They worshipped alongside men. They were instructed alongside men. They joined men in the public confession of sins and brought offerings to the house of the Lord. They could make religious vows like a man or enter the temple to pray. They ministered in the entrance of the house of God and in a variety of other service ministries in the spiritual life of Israel. God used women to exhort men in their spiritual walk and challenge them in their role as spiritual leaders. He gifted them with prophetic gifts and used them to deliver His people from their enemies. Clearly, women played a vital role in the spiritual life of Israel.

Despite these many avenues of ministry, the spiritual leadership of the nation fell to man at this period of history. This was not for cultural reasons but by the choice of God to call men to this position.

For Consideration:

What freedom did women have to worship and serve the Lord in the Old Testament? Give some examples.

Give some examples of women who encouraged or exhorted men in their position as spiritual leader? Was this right for them to do? Does exhorting or correcting a person in authority mean that we are not in subjection to their leadership?

Give some examples of women who were used by God to bring deliverance to His people?

How does the Law of Moses protect the headship of the male spiritual leaders?

Does the fact that God ordained a male spiritual leadership imply an oppression of women? Were men also to submit to the spiritual leadership God has established over them?

Does headship imply position of privilege or responsibility of service? If headship is the responsibility to care for those to whom it is responsible, then can we say that the spiritual head is more important than those it serves?

For Prayer:

Thank the Lord for the freedom He gave to women who worship and serve Him in the Old Testament. Take a moment to thank the Lord for the women He has used in your life to exhort you and draw you closer to Himself.

Ask the Lord to give you a proper perspective on headship in the Scripture. Ask Him to teach you to respect and honour those who care for your spiritual well-being.

Ask God to forgive you for times you have tried to take authority that was not yours to take. Ask Him to give you contentment to walk in His purpose for your life.

CHAPTER 3 -

JESUS AND WOMEN

One of the first references we have in the New Testament to the attitude of Jesus toward woman is seen in the Sermon on the Mount where He said:

27 "You have heard that it was said, 'You shall not commit adultery.' 28 But I say to you that everyone who looks at a woman with lustful intent has already committed adultery with her in his heart. (Matthew 5)

Jesus told men that if they were to look lustfully at a woman they were guilty before God of committing adultery in their hearts. In this statement He attacks the evils of pornography and lustful thoughts. He commanded men to be respectful in how they thought and responded to women with dignity and respect.

In Deuteronomy 24 we read:

1 "When a man takes a wife and marries her, if then she finds no favor in his eyes because he has found some indecency in her, and he writes her a certificate of divorce

and puts it in her hand and sends her out of his house,
and she departs out of his house (Deuteronomy 24)

Notice how the Law of Moses permitted a man to divorce his wife when she "found no favour in his eyes," or when he found something "indecent in her." The question of what this meant was open to great debate in the Old Testament. This lead to men divorcing their wives for a variety of reasons, leaving them for fend for themselves without support and income.

Jesus addressed this matter in the Sermon on the Mount when He said:

31 "It was also said, 'Whoever divorces his wife, let him give her a certificate of divorce.' 32 But I say to you that everyone who divorces his wife, except on the ground of sexual immorality, makes her commit adultery, and whoever marries a divorced woman commits adultery. (Matthew 5)

According to Jesus, a man was to remain with his wife and support her. He was not to divorce her unless she was guilty of sexual infidelity. Jesus protects women from being sent away because a husband lost interest in her. He expected that a man who, in that culture, was the bread winner, provide for the needs of his wife despite their disagreements. He was to honour her and his commitment to her. It is clear from this teaching of Jesus that women had the right to be treated with dignity and respect.

In Matthew 26.6-13 Jesus was in the home of Simon the leper when a woman anointed his feet with a very expensive perfume. The disciples took offence at the waste of a precious perfume. Jesus, however, took the side of the woman and defended her actions.

10 But Jesus, aware of this, said to them, "Why do you trouble the woman? For she has done a beautiful thing to me. (Matthew 26)

Luke 7 describes a time when Jesus was in the home of a Pharisee when a "woman of the city, who was a sinner," approached him and anointed his feet, kissed them and wiped them with her hair. The Pharisees were appalled at her behaviour and could not believe that Jesus would let such a woman even touch Him. Again, Jesus took her defence:

44 Then turning toward the woman he said to Simon, "Do you see this woman? I entered your house; you gave me no water for my feet, but she has wet my feet with her tears and wiped them with her hair. 45 You gave me no kiss, but from the time I came in she has not ceased to kiss my feet. 46 You did not anoint my head with oil, but she has anointed my feet with ointment. 47 Therefore I tell you, her sins, which are many, are forgiven—for she loved much. But he who is forgiven little, loves little." 48 And he said to her, "Your sins are forgiven." (Luke 7)

Jesus attacked the attitude of the men toward this woman and showed them how her actions were more noble then theirs. He did not hinder her from approaching Him. He accepted her, despite her reputation in the community. He loved her and accepted her offering. To Jesus, she was more sincere and loving than any man in that room.

In Luke 10 were read the story of two sisters by the name of Mary and Martha. They welcomed Jesus into their home. Martha kept very busy serving Jesus and the disciples while Mary sat at Jesus' feet listening to his teaching (Luke 10:39).

Eventually, Martha began to feel angry that Mary was leaving all the work of serving the guests to her. She interrupted Jesus' and asked Him to tell Mary to help her serve these guests.

40 But Martha was distracted with much serving. And she went up to him and said, "Lord, do you not care that my sister has left me to serve alone? Tell her then to help me." (Luke 10)

Jesus told Martha, however, that Mary was doing the right thing. He would not ask her to leave His side to busy herself with the duties of serving the guests.

41 But the Lord answered her, "Martha, Martha, you are anxious and troubled about many things, 42 but one thing is necessary. Mary has chosen the good portion, which will not be taken away from her." (Luke 10)

Jesus recognised Mary as an intelligent human being who was interested in learning the truth. He accepted her as His student. She had every right to sit at His feet like the men around her to learn. Jesus did not send Mary to the kitchen to serve the guests. He delighted in her presence as a student of the Word He taught.

In John 4 we see Jesus in a religious discussion with a Samaritan woman. They discussed the difference between the Samaritan and Jewish understanding of worship. They also touched on the issue of the Messiah who was to come. When the disciples, who had been shopping, returned to Jesus and found him in a deep discussion with a Samaritan woman they were surprised:

27 Just then his disciples came back. They marveled that he was talking with a woman, but no one said, "What do you seek?" or, "Why are you talking with her?" (John 4)

Notice from verse 27 that the disciples marvelled that Jesus was talking with a woman. No mention is made here in this verse about the fact that she was a Samaritan. Jesus had entered a theological debate with a woman. The disciples found Jesus freely conversing with this woman about deep issues. He allowed her to question Him and in turn responded to her questions. Jesus saw her as an intelligent human being, fully capable of learning and discussing spiritual matters. This was quite radical for the day.

In John 8.1-11 the Pharisees brought a woman caught in the act of adultery to Jesus. They were using this woman to find a way to condemn Him. The interesting thing about this scene is that we have no mention of the man who was caught with her. The Law of Moses was very clear that both the man and the woman were to be put to death:

10 "If a man commits adultery with the wife of his neighbor, both the adulterer and the adulteress shall surely be put to death. (Leviticus 20)

Knowing the intentions of the Pharisees, Jesus responded by saying: "Let him who is without sin among you be the first to throw a stone at her" (John 8:7). One by one they left the woman alone with Jesus. When everyone had left Jesus spoke to the adulteress woman:

10 Jesus stood up and said to her, "Woman, where are they? Has no one condemned you?" 11 She said, "No one, Lord." And Jesus said, "Neither do I condemn you; go, and from now on sin no more." (John 8)

Jesus saw the hypocrisy of the Pharisees and knew that they were guilty before God as well. If this woman deserved to die for sinning against God, then so did the Pharisees. Jesus did not treat her any differently because she was a woman.

Jesus saw both men and woman on an equal standing when it came to their need for forgiveness and salvation. Speaking to the men who looked down on the "woman of the city, who was a sinner" in Luke 7:37, Jesus said:

47 Therefore I tell you, her sins, which are many, are forgiven—for she loved much. But he who is forgiven little, loves little." 48 And he said to her, "Your sins are forgiven." 49 Then those who were at table with him began to say among themselves, "Who is this, who even forgives sins?" 50 And he said to the woman, "Your faith has saved you; go in peace." (Luke 7)

While the men present in that room refused to accept her, Jesus assured her that God had accepted her. She could go her way knowing that her salvation and forgiveness had been guaranteed.

The religious leaders of the day condemned Jesus for healing a woman on the Sabbath day (Luke 13). Jesus defended his actions before these leaders saying:

15 Then the Lord answered him, "You hypocrites! Does not each of you on the Sabbath untie his ox or his donkey from the manger and lead it away to water it? 16 And ought not this woman, a daughter of Abraham whom Satan bound for eighteen years, be loosed from this bond on the Sabbath day?" (Luke 13)

The men present that day would treat their donkey better than a woman. They would break the Sabbath law to feed and water their donkey but would not lift a hand to help a woman in need on the Sabbath. Jesus calls these men hypocrites. Notice how Jesus addressed the woman. He calls her a "daughter of Abraham." In calling her a daughter of Abraham, he is identifying her with the covenant made with Abraham. She was a partner with men in the salvation that would come through that covenantal agreement. She had an equal standing in salvation. She was an equal covenant partner with men in the promise God made through Abraham.

In His teaching, the Lord often used illustrations that could be understood by the women of His day. He used the illustration of a woman mixing yeast into flour to describe the kingdom of God (see Matthew 13.33). On another occasion he told a parable about a woman sweeping out her house to find a lost coin (Luke 15.8). Still on another occasion he spoke about two women grinding at a mill to illustrate what would happen in the last days (Matthew 24.41).

The use of these illustrations shows us that Jesus wanted to include women in his teaching. He often spoke to a mixed crowd. He was sensitive to both women and men in His teaching.

We understand from Matthew 27:55 and Luke 8:3 that a group of women followed Jesus and his disciples as they preached the gospel. These women contributed greatly to His ministry:

55 There were also many women there, looking on from a distance, who had followed Jesus from Galilee, ministering to him, 56 among whom were Mary Magdalene

*and Mary the mother of James and Joseph and the
mother of the sons of Zebedee. (Matthew 27)*

*1 Soon afterward he went on through cities and villages,
proclaiming and bringing the good news of the kingdom
of God. And the twelve were with him, 2 and also some
women who had been healed of evil spirits and infirmi-
ties: Mary, called Magdalene, from whom seven demons
had gone out, 3 and Joanna, the wife of Chuza, Herod's
household manager, and Susanna, and many others,
who provided for them out of their means. (Luke 8)*

These women ministered to Jesus as He and His disciples
travelled from place to place. They gave financially and
practically to Jesus out of their own resources.

When the Lord Jesus was crucified, women prepared
spices and ointments for His burial:

*55 The women who had come with him from Galilee fol-
lowed and saw the tomb and how his body was laid. 56
Then they returned and prepared spices and ointments.
On the Sabbath they rested according to the commandment. (Luke 23)*

In John 20.10-18 we read how Mary Magdalene discovered the empty tomb of Jesus and announced this to the
disciples:

*1 Now on the first day of the week Mary Magdalene came
to the tomb early, while it was still dark, and saw that the
stone had been taken away from the tomb. 2 So she ran
and went to Simon Peter and the other disciple, the one
whom Jesus loved, and said to them, "They have taken
the Lord out of the tomb, and we do not know where they
have laid him." (John 20)*

While her understanding of the events was incorrect, Jesus would meet her at the tomb and reveal Himself personally to her.

11 But Mary stood weeping outside the tomb, and as she wept she stooped to investigate the tomb. 12 And she saw two angels in white, sitting where the body of Jesus had lain, one at the head and one at the feet. 13 They said to her, "Woman, why are you weeping?" She said to them, "They have taken away my Lord, and I do not know where they have laid him." 14 Having said this, she turned around and saw Jesus standing, but she did not know that it was Jesus. 15 Jesus said to her, "Woman, why are you weeping? Whom are you seeking?" Supposing him to be the gardener, she said to him, "Sir, if you have carried him away, tell me where you have laid him, and I will take him away." 16 Jesus said to her, "Mary." She turned and said to him in Aramaic, "Rabboni!" (which means Teacher). 17 Jesus said to her, "Do not cling to me, for I have not yet ascended to the Father; but go to my brothers and say to them, 'I am ascending to my Father and your Father, to my God and your God.'" 18 Mary Magdalene went and announced to the disciples, "I have seen the Lord"—and that he had said these things to her.
(John 20)

Jesus commissioned Mary to announce His resurrection and ascension. What a privilege it was to announce the greatest event in history. This resurrection and ascension would bring salvation to the ends of the earth. There was never a more important message to proclaim. "He is risen victorious over sin and death. He is ascended to sit at the right hand of the Father on high." Jesus entrusted this message to Mary Magdalene.

Jesus held women in high regard. He taught that woman should be respected and treated with dignity. He showed no partiality in justice. Men and women were equals before the law in the mind of Jesus. He taught women and men together and made no distinction in their intellectual abilities. According to Jesus, both men and women were equal partners in salvation. Women ministered to Jesus and were commissioned by Him to announce the good news of the gospel.

Divorce, in the New Testament would not be as easy. Men would not be able to divorce their wives for any reason. Wrong, lustful thoughts about women were forbidden and seen on a par with adultery. By His example, Jesus stretched the cultural boundaries regarding the place and role of women.

What is important to note, however, is that while Christ elevated the position of women and used them in the proclamation of the gospel, He still placed the leadership of the church in the hands of men. He did not choose women for the role of apostle or disciple. In this regard, Jesus respected the principle of male headship, taught in the Old Testament. While we may speculate as to why this is the case, He is our example and reveals to us the purpose of God for the early church.

For Consideration:

What does the Sermon on the Mount teach us about how Jesus held women in high regard?

On numerous occasions Jesus took up the defence of women when they were mistreated or accused by the men of His day. What does this teach us about the importance of justice and truth over gender?

Jesus openly taught and debated with women of His day. He also used illustrations in His teaching that the women of His day could related to. What does this say us about how He viewed their intellectual ability?

Jesus commissioned Mary Magdalene to tell the disciples about His resurrection and ascension? Why was this message significant? What does it teach us about the equality of men and women in the sharing of the Gospel?

Is it significant that despite the high regard in which Jesus held women, He did not choose women to be among His twelve disciples?

For Prayer:

Have you ever found yourself showing favouritism based on gender? Ask the Lord to forgive you and help you to see everyone for the qualities God has given them.

Consider the conversations Jesus has with women who were treated as outcasts in their society. Thank the Lord that He accepts us as we are, male or female, saint or sinner.

Ask the Lord to help us to accept His purpose for the church and its leadership. Ask Him to reveal the purpose He has for you personally.

CHAPTER 4 -

THE EARLY CHURCH

Women played a significant role in the early church in the days of the apostles. Both men and women came to faith in the Lord Jesus and were being added to the church.

14 And more than ever believers were added to the Lord, multitudes of both men and women (Acts 5)

It is important to note the phrase "were added to the Lord." Both men and women were added to the list of believers becoming part of the church. There is no distinction made between the sexes. This may not strike us as significant in our culture and time but let's compare this verse with other passages in Scripture. Consider Matthew 14:21 and Matthew 15:38 for example.

21 And those who ate were about five thousand men, besides women and children. (Matthew 14)

38 Those who ate were four thousand men, besides women and children. (Matthew 15)

Notice in these verses that the men alone are numbered. The women and children were not counted at that time. Consider also the story of the children of Jacob who travelled to the safety of Egypt because of a great famine. The number of those who arrived in Egypt is recorded for us in Genesis 46:26-27;

26 All the persons belonging to Jacob who came into Egypt, who were his own descendants, not including Jacob's sons' wives, were sixty-six persons in all. 27 And the sons of Joseph, who were born to him in Egypt, were two. All the persons of the house of Jacob who came into Egypt were seventy. (Genesis 46)

A close examination of this passage will show us that the only way you can get seventy people from the list of those who arrived in Egypt is by omitting the women and children. In fact, two sisters mentioned in verse 15 and verse 17 (Dinah and Serah) are not counted. Verse 26 tells us that the number of those who travelled to Egypt did not include the wives of Jacob's sons.

In the church of the New Testament, women were numbered with the men. They were equal partners and members of the body of Christ.

From Acts 2:17-18 we understand that this partnership in salvation extended to the outpouring of the Holy Spirit. According to Peter, the Holy Spirit would be poured out on both men and women.

*17 "'And in the last days it shall be, God declares,
that I will pour out my Spirit on all flesh,
and your sons and your daughters shall prophesy,
and your young men shall see visions,
and your old men shall dream dreams;
18 even on my male servants and female servants
in those days I will pour out my Spirit, and they shall
prophesy. (Acts 2)*

Another sign of this equality is seen in the fact that both men and women are now permitted the covenantal sign of baptism.

12 But when they believed Philip as he preached good news about the kingdom of God and the name of Jesus Christ, they were baptized, both men and women. (Acts 8)

Notice in Acts 8:12 that both men and women were baptised. As you may recall, under the Old Testament, it was the young men only who were circumcised as a sign of the covenant. Women did not have a sign of identification with the God of Abraham, Isaac and Jacob. This was to change under the new covenant. Both men and women were baptised. They are now equal partners in the sign of baptism.

Women joined men in prayer, worship and Bible instruction in the New Testament church.

13 And when they had entered, they went up to the upper room, where they were staying, Peter and John and James and Andrew, Philip and Thomas, Bartholomew and Matthew, James the son of Alphaeus and Simon the Zealot and Judas the son of James. 14 All these with one accord were devoting themselves to prayer, together with the women and Mary the mother of Jesus, and his brothers. (Acts 1)

The apostles gathered with women in the upper room to pray. Notice in verse 14 how they devoted themselves to prayer, together with the women. The implication here is that this was not just a one-time event but a regular occurrence.

When persecution broke out in the early church under Saul, both women and men were being dragged off to prison for their faith in Jesus Christ:

3 But Saul was ravaging the church, and entering house after house, he dragged off men and women and commit-ted them to prison. (Acts 8)

1 But Saul, still breathing threats and murder against the disciples of the Lord, went to the high priest 2 and asked him for letters to the synagogues at Damascus, so that if he found any belonging to the Way, men or women, he might bring them bound to Jerusalem. (Acts 9)

4 I persecuted this Way to the death, binding and deliver-ing to prison both men and women (Acts 22)

Paul expressed his deep gratitude for both Aquila and his wife Priscilla who risked their lives for him and the cause of the gospel.

3 Greet Prisca and Aquila, my fellow workers in Christ Je-sus, 4 who risked their necks for my life, to whom not only I give thanks but all the churches of the Gentiles give thanks as well. (Romans 16)

Notice how Paul recognized both Aquila and Priscilla as being his "fellow workers in Christ Jesus." He makes no distinction because of sex. Both were equally valuable in the work of the Gospel.

The New Testament commends several women who worked hard for the cause of the gospel. Paul sends his greetings to Tryphaena and Tryphosa who worked hard for the Lord.

12 Greet those workers in the Lord, Tryphaena and Tryphosa. Greet the beloved Persis, who has worked hard in the Lord. (Romans 16)

He would also exhort Euodia and Syntyche to agree and challenged the church to help these women who had laboured "side by side" with him in the gospel.

2 I entreat Euodia and I entreat Syntyche to agree in the Lord. 3 Yes, I ask you also, true companion, help these women, who have labored side by side with me in the gospel with Clement and the rest of my fellow workers, whose names are in the book of life. (Philippians 4)

The women of the early church were involved in many different aspects of church life. Writing to Titus the apostle Paul would instruct him to encourage the older women of the congregation to be active in the role teaching and admonishing younger women.

3 Older women likewise are to be reverent in behavior, not slanderers or slaves to much wine. They are to teach what is good, 4 and so train the young women to love their husbands and children, 5 to be self-controlled, pure, working at home, kind, and submissive to their own husbands, that the word of God may not be reviled. (Titus 2)

The experience of these older women was a great asset to the church. They rubbed shoulders with the younger women and shared insights with them, helping them to be what God had called them to be. The support and advice of these more experienced women would have been a tremendous blessing to these young mothers and wives.

Paul encouraged Timothy not to neglect the care of the widows in his church. There was, however, some question as to what widows should be added to the list for church assistance.

Writing to Timothy as the pastor of the church in Ephesus, Paul gave a list of qualifications for widows who were supported by the church.

9 Let a widow be enrolled if she is not less than sixty years of age, having been the wife of one husband, 10 and having a reputation for good works: if she has brought up children, has shown hospitality, has washed the feet of the saints, has cared for the afflicted, and has devoted herself to every good work. (1 Timothy 5)

The widows the church supported needed to have a reputation for good work, hospitality and servant attitude. They were to have brought up their family well and demonstrated care for those who were afflicted. These qualities were necessary because these widows would likely continue serving the Lord in these ways while being supported by the church. This shows us also that women in the early church were involved in ministries of hospitality, charity and compassion.

In 2 Timothy 1.5 Paul commended both Timothy's grandmother and mother for having passed on their faith to the young Timothy.

5 I am reminded of your sincere faith, a faith that dwelt first in your grandmother Lois and your mother Eunice and now, I am sure, dwells in you as well. (2 Timothy 1)

Paul recognised that a big part of what Timothy had become, had to do with the spiritual instruction and upbringing he had received from his mother and grandmother at home. These women were instrumental in bringing up a child who would serve the Lord as pastor and companion to the apostle Paul.

In Acts 18 we read the story of a man by the name of Apollos.

24 Now a Jew named Apollos, a native of Alexandria, came to Ephesus. He was an eloquent man, competent in the Scriptures. 25 He had been instructed in the way of the Lord. And being fervent in spirit, he spoke and taught accurately the things concerning Jesus, though he knew only the baptism of John. 26 He began to speak boldly in the synagogue, but when Priscilla and Aquila heard him, they took him aside and explained to him the way of God more accurately. 27 And when he wished to cross to Achaia, the brothers encouraged him and wrote to the disciples to welcome him. When he arrived, he greatly helped those who through grace had believed, 28 for he powerfully refuted the Jews in public, showing by the Scriptures that the Christ was Jesus. (Acts 18)

Apollos was an eloquent man who spoke very well. Notice, however, that when Aquila and his wife Priscilla heard him they took him aside to explain the way of God "more accurately." The context indicates that both Aquila and Priscilla had a role to play in the discipling of Apollos. The result was that Apollos became a great help to those who believed (verse 27). Priscilla worked alongside of her husband in equipping Apollos for greater and more effective service.

Acts 9 tells the story of a woman by the name of Tabitha or Dorcas:

36 Now there was in Joppa a disciple named Tabitha, which, translated, means Dorcas. She was full of good

*works and acts of charity. 37 In those days she became
ill and died, and when they had washed her, they laid her
in an upper room. 38 Since Lydda was near Joppa, the
disciples, hearing that Peter was there, sent two men to
him, urging him, "Please come to us without delay." 39
So Peter rose and went with them. And when he arrived,
they took him to the upper room. All the widows stood beside him weeping and showing tunics and other garments
that Dorcas made while she was with them. (Acts 9)*

Tabitha is called a disciple in verse 36. In other words, she
was a follower of the Lord Jesus. Notice how she served
the Lord Jesus— "she was full of good works and acts of
charity" (verse 36). From verse 39 we learn that as a seam-
stress, she had sewn many articles of clothing and distrib-
uted them to the widows in her community. When she died,
her presence was greatly missed. The widows wept and
showed tunics and garments to the disciples that Dorcas
had made for them in their time of need.

While women were very busy in various aspects of church
ministry, there no clear evidence in the New Testament
that the early church ever had an official role of deaconess.
There are only two references in the New Testament which
could possibly indicate such an office in the church. The
first of these references is in 1 Timothy 3. Speaking about
the qualifications of deacons, the apostle Paul told Timothy:

*8 Deacons likewise must be dignified, not double-
tongued, not addicted to much wine, not greedy for dis-
honest gain. 9 They must hold the mystery of the faith
with a clear conscience. 10 And let them also be tested
first; then let them serve as deacons if they prove themselves blameless. 11 Their wives likewise must be*

dignified, not slanderers, but sober-minded, faithful in all things. (1Timothy 3)

Paul was instructing Timothy in these verse about the qualifications of the men who exercise the role of deacon in the church. In verse eleven the apostle reminds Timothy that the wives of deacons needed to demonstrate certain qualities. The idea is that if the wife of the deacon was a slanderer or unfaithful to him, this would have a devastating impact on his witness in the community and affect his ability to minister as a servant of God.

There are those who interpret verse 11 to mean that the church also recognized women as deacons. They base this on the fact that these women are mentioned in the context of Paul speaking about deacons and their qualifications. The problem, with this, however, is that the passage makes it quite clear both in the English translations and in the Greek that Paul is speaking about the wives of deacons and not about an official role in the church. The word "deacon" is not used in reference to women in this verse. The Greek word used here is the word *"gunaikós"*, which is literally translated by the word woman or wife.

The second problem with seeing in verse 11 a reference to women deacons, comes in the very next verse where Paul goes on to explain what he means:

12 Let deacons each be the husband of one wife, managing their children and their own households well. (1 Timothy 3)

The fact that Paul says that a deacon was to be a husband of one wife makes it clear that he is referring to male deacons in this section of Scripture. Second, and more importantly in this context is that Paul told Timothy that the

reason the wife needed to be of noble character was because if she wasn't it may disqualify her husband from the
role of deacon. The husband was to manage his household well. If his children or his wife were unruly, unfaithful
or living ungodly lives, then this man should very likely
cease being a deacon and focus on his own family.

The only other passage used to support the role of deaconess in the New Testament church is Romans 16.1:

*1 I commend to you our sister Phoebe, a servant of the
church at Cenchreae, 2 that you may welcome her in the
Lord in a way worthy of the saints, and help her in whatever she may need from you, for she has been a patron
of many and of myself as well. (Romans 16)*

Writing to the Romans the apostle commends a sister by
the name of Phoebe. He describes her as a servant of the
church at Cenchreae (verse 1). The word the apostle uses
here for servant is the Greek word "*diákonos*" from which
we get the word deacon. The word "diákonos" is translated
in English by the word minister, servant or deacon. There
are those who interpret this verse to mean that Phoebe
was a deaconess. We need to be very careful about making this assumption however. Let's consider, for example,
other uses of the Greek word "*diákonos*" in the New Testament.

Listen to the instructions of Jesus in Matthew 23:

*9 And call no man your father on earth, for you have one
Father, who is in heaven. 10 Neither be called instructors,
for you have one instructor, the Christ. 11 The greatest
among you shall be your servant. 12 Whoever exalts himself will be humbled, and whoever humbles himself will
be exalted. (Matthew 23)*

Speaking about those who wanted to be recognized in their community, Jesus told His disciples that the one who wanted to be greatest was to be a servant (diákonos). In other words, Jesus was telling us that we all need to deacons in the sense that we are servants of the body of Christ. Jesus is not speaking here about an official position in the church but a role of servanthood.

In John 2:5 the Lord Jesus was at the wedding of Cana. When they ran out of wine, His mother told the servants present to do whatever Jesus asked them to do. The word used here to speak of the servants who served wine is the Greek word "diákonos". They were individuals who cared for the needs of others in this secular event, but they were not deacons in an official capacity in the church.

We read in Romans 13

1 Let every person be subject to the governing authorities. For there is no authority except from God, and those that exist have been instituted by God. 2 Therefore whoever resists the authorities resists what God has appointed, and those who resist will incur judgment. 3 For rulers are not a terror to good conduct, but to bad. Would you have no fear of the one who is in authority? Then do what is good, and you will receive his approval, 4 for he is God's servant for your good. But if you do wrong, be afraid, for he does not bear the sword in vain. For he is the servant of God, an avenger who carries out God's wrath on the wrongdoer. (Romans 13)

In this passage, the apostle Paul challenges believers to submit to the governing authorities in their secular government. Notice particularly in verse 4 that Paul told the Romans that the one who is in governmental authority over them was God's servant (diákonos). Once again, we see the use of the Greek word "diákonos" referring to a civil servant but not to an official role in the church.

There are many other times in the New Testament where the word "diákonos" is uses to refer simply to a servant and not to the role of church deacon (see also 2 Corinthians 3:6; 2 Corinthians 11:23; Galatians 2:17). The use of the word "diákonos" in Romans 16:1 in connection with Phoebe is not solid proof that the early church recognized her as a deaconess in an official capacity.

While women did minister in service roles in the context of the early church, there is no clear indication in the New Testament that there was at this time a recognised position of deaconess. Any argument for the role of deaconess must be based on the roles women played in the life of the church. While there is no clear example of a recognised position of deaconess in the New Testament church, there are certainly many examples of women who fulfilled the role in practice through their deeds of compassion, charity, hospitality and instruction of younger women and children.

While the position of deaconess is unclear, the New Testament church did recognize the role prophetesses. We have a clear example of this in Acts 21, when Paul went to visit the home of Philip the evangelist:

8 On the next day we departed and came to Caesarea, and we entered the house of Philip the evangelist, who was one of the seven, and stayed with him. 9 He had four unmarried daughters, who prophesied. (Acts 21)

Mention is made here of Philip's four unmarried daughters who prophesied. It should be understood here that the gift of prophecy was exercised in various ways in the Bible.

We have, for example, the case of Miriam, the sister of Moses who was a prophetess and used her prophetic gift through music:

20 Then Miriam the prophetess, the sister of Aaron, took a tambourine in her hand, and all the women went out after her with tambourines and dancing. 21 And Miriam sang to them:

"Sing to the Lord, for he has triumphed gloriously; the horse and his rider he has thrown into the sea." (Exodus 15)

Philip's daughters were recognized as prophetesses in Acts 21:9. We do not know how the Lord used them in this ministry, but it is quite clear that they were His instruments to communicate His character and purpose to the church. This was a recognised role for women.

1 Corinthians 11 makes is clear that the prophetess had a role to play in the life of the church. Here in this passage the apostle gave instruction to the church of Corinth about women who prayed and prophesied in worship:

3 But I want you to understand that the head of every man is Christ, the head of a wife is her husband, and the head of Christ is God. 4 Every man who prays or prophesies with his head covered dishonors his head, 5 but every wife who prays or prophesies with her head uncovered dishonors her head, since it is the same as if her head were shaven. (1 Corinthians 11)

It is not my purpose in the context of this chapter to enter a discussion of head coverings. What is important for us to note is that Paul speaks about women praying and prophesying. He does not condemn this practice but recognized that it was very normal for women to be involved in prayer and prophecy in the church. His only concern is that women cover their head a sign of respect. Notice from verses 8-10 that the respect she was to offer was based on the fact that man was the firstborn and she had been created to be a helper: (Genesis 2:18):

8 For man was not made from woman, but woman from man. 9 Neither was man created for woman, but woman for man. 10 That is why a wife ought to have a symbol of authority on her head, because of the angels. (1 Corinthians 11)

This covering on her head was a "symbol of authority" and showed her willingness to be in submission to those God had placed in authority in the church.

The role of prophecy in the early church, according to Paul one of strengthening, encouraging and comforting the body of Christ (see 1 Corinthians 14.3). Through this gift of prophecy, women were able to strengthen, comfort and encourage the body of Christ.

Women worked hard for the cause of the gospel in the New Testament. They joined men in worship, prayer, and instruction in the Word of God. They suffered for their faith and were persecuted alongside of men for their stand. They devoted themselves to ministries of compassion, charity, hospitality and the teaching of other women to walk in the purpose of God. While we cannot prove clearly from Scripture that the early church had an official office of deaconess, Scriptures certainly exhort women to exercise a service role in the body. Those who had received a prophetic word for the strengthening, encouragement or comfort of the body were given freedom to speak that word to the body. They were to exercise this role, however, in a manner that was respectful to the leadership God had established in the church.

For Consideration:

What evidence do we have in the New Testament that men and women are equal when it comes to salvation?

While circumcision, as the Old Testament sign of the covenant was for men only, we discover in the New Testament that the covenant sign of baptism was for both men and women. What does this tell us about the equality of both men and women in salvation and partnership in the gospel?

List some of the work in which women of the New Testament church were involved.

While there is no clear evidenced of an official position of female deacons in the New Testament, women were involved in a variety of service ministries. Is it important that we have a title in our service for the Lord?

What is prophecy? How could this gift be used? What was its purpose?

Why did Paul encourage women who prayed and prophesied to wear a head covering? How does the apostle draw

this conclusion from the story of creation and God's purpose for man and woman?

For Prayer:

Thank the Lord that there is no distinction between male
or female, rich or poor, religious or secular when it comes
to salvation. The Lord Jesus is willing to save all who will
come to Him.

Take a moment to consider the role of the godly Christian
women in your church and community. Thank the Lord for
their impact on your life and the lives of many around them.

Ask the Lord to help you (whether you be male or female)
to be submissive to the order He has established in your
church and community.

Ask God to give you grace to live and serve Him whether
your efforts are recognized or not.

CHAPTER 5 -

THE TEACHING OF PAUL

IN 1 CORINTHIANS 11

It is at this point that we come to the teaching of the apostle Paul. His instruction about the role of women in the ministry of the church can be found in three main passages (1 Corinthians 11, 1 Corinthians 14 and 1 Timothy 2). We will take the time to examine each of these passages individually. In this chapter we will look at what Paul says in 1 Corinthians 11:2-16.

1 Corinthians 11 begins with both a commendation and an exhortation to the church in Corinth:

2 Now I commend you because you remember me in everything and maintain the traditions even as I delivered them to you. 3 But I want you to understand that the head of every man is Christ, the head of a wife is her husband, and the head of Christ is God. (1 Corinthians 11)

Let's first consider the commendation of the apostle in verse 1. This sets the tone for what Paul wants to say.

Notice how he commends the Corinthians because they remembered him in everything and maintained the traditions as he had delivered them to the church.

The word "tradition" used here by Paul seems to refer to teaching about acceptable practice. We have numerous examples of the use of this word in the New Testament. In Matthew 15 the Pharisees and Scribes came to Jesus with a question:

> 1 Then Pharisees and scribes came to Jesus from Jerusalem and said, 2 "Why do your disciples break the tradition of the elders? For they do not wash their hands when they eat." (Matthew 15)

The word tradition in verse 1 is the same word used by Paul in 1 Corinthians 11:2. The concern of these religious leaders was that they saw these rough disciples eating without first ceremonially washing their hands, as was the tradition of the elders. This tradition was not found in the written Scriptures or the Law of Moses but was a supplemental law added by the religious leaders of the day.

Listen to the response of Jesus to these leaders:

> 3 He answered them, "And why do you break the commandment of God for the sake of your tradition? 4 For God commanded, 'Honor your father and your mother,' and, 'Whoever reviles father or mother must surely die.' 5 But you say, 'If anyone tells his father or his mother, "What you would have gained from me is given to God," 6 he need not honor his father.' So for the sake of your tradition you have made void the word of God. (Matthew 15)

Jesus accuses the Pharisees and scribes of breaking the commandment of God for the sake of their "tradition." He gives an example of this in verses 4-5 about how they treated their mother and father. He concludes with the statement: "For the sake of your tradition you have made void the word of God" (verse 5b).

Writing about this same incident, Mark would record Jesus as saying:

8 You leave the commandment of God and hold to the tradition of men."9 And he said to them, "You have a fine way of rejecting the commandment of God in order to establish your tradition! (Mark 7)

Writing to the Colossians, the apostle Paul would say:

8 See to it that no one takes you captive by philosophy and empty deceit, according to human tradition, according to the elemental spirits of the world, and not according to Christ. (Colossians 2)

From these passages we see that there is a distinction made between the traditions of man or the traditions of the elders and the clear commands of God.

Having said this, we need to understand that there are some traditions that we are encouraged to maintain simply because they honour God and His purposes. In 1 Corinthians 11:2 Paul commends the church of Corinth for remembering the traditions he passed on to them. Writing to the Thessalonians the apostle would say:

15 So then, brothers, stand firm and hold to the traditions that you were taught by us, either by our spoken word or by our letter. (2 Thessalonians 2)

*6 Now we command you, brothers, in the name of our
Lord Jesus Christ, that you keep away from any brother
who is walking in idleness and not in accord with the tradition that you received from us. (2 Thessalonians 3)*

The apostle makes it very clear that there are some traditions that should be maintained. In fact, notice from 2
Thessalonians 3:6, Paul encouraged believers to keep
away from a brother who was not walking according to the
tradition they had received through the teaching of the
apostles.

The traditions the apostle speaks about in 1 Corinthians
11:2 seem to refer to proper practices in the church and
Christian life that help maintain unity in the body and bring
honour to God. Paul commends the church of Corinth for
remembering these traditions he has taught them. He
does, however, have one concern for the church. That
concern is expressed in 1 Corinthians 11:3:

*3 But I want you to understand that the head of every
man is Christ, the head of a wife is her husband, and the
head of Christ is God. (1 Corinthians 11)*

According to the apostle Paul there was an order that God
had established in the life of the church. Paul states in
verse 11 that God is the head of all and to Him we must all
submit. Christ, as the Son of God, submitted to the purpose of the Father and laid down His life in obedience to
the Father's will. Man submits to Christ and is accountable
to Him as the head of his family and manager of the earth's
resources. Finally, woman (or a wife), submits to man
(husband), as his helper. It is important to note that submission does not mean that we are less important. Christ
is equal to the Father in every way. His submission to the
Father's will does not make Him less than the Father. In a

similar way, woman is equal to man and her submission to him does not make her less than man.

Having stated this God-ordained order, Paul now moves on to speak of how this order was to work itself out in the service of the church:

4 Every man who prays or prophesies with his head cov- ered dishonors his head, 5 but every wife who prays or prophesies with her head uncovered dishonors her head, since it is the same as if her head were shaven. (1 Corin- thians 11)

In verses 4 and 5 Paul speaks about praying and prophe- sying in a public setting. What is important for us to note is that both men and women were permitted to do this. The only difference between a man and a woman praying or prophesying in public was that the woman was to cover her head when she did so.

Paul would go on in verses 4 to say that if a man prayed or prophesied with his head covered he dishonoured his head. There is some confusion as to what Paul is saying here. Remember, however, that in the context the head of man was Christ. In other word, when a man prayed or prophesied with his head covered he showed disrespect for Christ, his head.

In verse 2 Paul began by reminding us that he was speak- ing about traditions. In the culture in which I grew up, it is customary for a man to take off his hat when he goes into to church. I have even been on worksites or sporting events where we have had prayer. As we began to pray, the men would remove their hats as a sign of respect to God. If a man went for a job interview, he would be sure to remove his hat as a sign of respect to the interviewer. If he were to enter someone's home, he would take off his hat in respect for the people of that home. This is the cultural tradition from which I have come.

What Paul appears to be telling the Corinthians is that if a man covers his head with a veil or hat of some kind when he prays or prophesied, he is not showing respect to Jesus his head. This, according to Paul was proper Christian etiquette.

Removing a head covering when in the presence of God was an obligation for a man but not so for a woman. If a woman did not wear a head-covering, she showed disrespect for her head. The head of woman, according to Paul, was man (verse 3).

There is an interesting passage in Song of Solomon 5. In the context of the chapter a man comes to the door of his beloved's chamber and knocks. She is unwilling to open the door for him, so he leaves. Laying there in bed, she realizes what she has done and has a change of heart. Putting on her clothes, she rushes out of the house to find him. Verses six and seven recount the story of what happened when she went out into the streets looking for her lover:

> 6 I opened to my beloved,
> but my beloved had turned and gone.
> My soul failed me when he spoke.
> I sought him, but found him not;
> I called him, but he gave no answer.
> 7 The watchmen found me
> as they went about in the city;
> they beat me, they bruised me,
> they took away my veil,
> those watchmen of the walls. (Song of Solomon 5)

As she roamed the streets at night, the city watchmen found her. Notice how they treated her in verse 7—they beat her and took away her veil. They shamed her and treated her with great disrespect. For these watchmen, only a prostitute would roam the streets at night. They treated her as a woman of the streets. Part of the disrespect shown for this woman was that they stripped her of her veil. This woman reserved herself for her lover –to be exposed to any other man was a great dishonour to her and to the man she loved.

While there is clearly in this teaching of Paul a cultural element, Paul also offers a theological reason for the use of the veil in verse 7-9:

7 For a man ought not to cover his head, since he is the image and glory of God, but woman is the glory of man. 8 For man was not made from woman, but woman from man. 9 Neither was man created for woman, but woman for man. 10 That is why a wife ought to have a symbol of authority on her head, because of the angels. (1 Corinthians 11)

Paul makes several points in verses 7-9 and ends with the statement in verse 10: "That is why a wife ought to have a symbol of authority on her head". Let's take a moment to examine these points.

In verse 7 the apostle says:

For a man ought not to cover his head, since he is the image and glory of God, but woman is the glory of man
(verse 7)

According to Paul, man is the image and glory of God, but woman is the glory of man. Notice first that the apostle speaks of man being the image of God. While both men and women were created in the image of God, man is described here as the image of God in verse 7. Paul does not attribute this quality to woman in this verse. This may be significant.

The word, "image" refers to a representation or reflection. While this reflection is not the real thing, it represents the person it reflects. In other words, man has been given the responsibility of being the representative of God and to reflect His image on this earth. It is true that both men and women must reflect the character of God, but Paul is telling us here in verse 7 that man has been given a charge by God as the head of his family to be his official representative.

Consider for a moment how your church functions. In your church you may have a pastor, who has been called of God to shepherd the flock. He has a title and spiritual obligation to assure the well-being of each member. This does not mean that no one else is involved in pastoral care in the church. There may be elders or deacons visiting the sick and caring for the needs of the congregation. There are also other members of the church who are caring for each other. In fact, everyone has an obligation toward each other. All are busy serving and ministering pastorally to each other. While everyone is ministering, you still have a pastor who is overseeing the work of the church. He bears the title and that title carries with it a special obligation before God. He is accountable to God not only to reflect His image to the flock but to see that each member of the church is growing in their ability to reflect God's image to the world. This is the obligation God has given to man.

As a representative of God, man has been given a glorious charge. God has honoured him with the responsibility of being His chosen representative in the world. It is his privilege to serve God in this way and as such he bears the honour and dignity of this position in the world, his family and his church. In this sense, he is the glory of God.

Paul goes on to say in verse 7 that woman is the glory of man. In saying this, Paul is not saying that women have any less standing before God, on the contrary, they are equally loved by God and equally filled by His Spirit. While man was given the responsibility to be God's representative, woman was given the responsibility to be a support and helper to him in this role. Her support and blessing give him strength to do what God has called him to do. Her God-given insight helps him maintain perspective. Her encouragement gives him strength to carry on. Her role is no less important than his. Her role also is a glorious one.

Why should man be the leader and representative and not woman? Paul tells us that it was because woman came from man.

For man was not made from woman, but woman from man" (verse 8)

Woman owes her life to man. God created her from man and breathed into her the breath of life.

What is significant in these words of Paul is that there is no reference to ability. There are those who speak about the differences between the sexes. They try, by this means, to show why a man is a better leader than woman because of these differences. The reality of the matter is that women are as capable of leadership as men. Paul tells us that the reason man is head is because he was created first and because God made woman from man to be a helper. Headship has nothing to do with ability. It has everything to do with God's choice.

Paul goes on in verse 9 to say:

Neither was man created for woman, but woman for man.
(verse 9)

Paul refers here to the creation of woman as recorded in Genesis 2:

20 The man gave names to all livestock and to the birds of the heavens and to every beast of the field. But for Adam there was not found a helper fit for him. 21 So the Lord God caused a deep sleep to fall upon the man, and while he slept took one of his ribs and closed up its place with flesh. 22 And the rib that the Lord God had taken from the man he made into a woman and brought her to the man. (Genesis 2)

God made woman to be a helper for Adam. This was the role given to her by God. It was in this role that she could become everything God intended her to become. Woman was uniquely created for this responsibility. Man would need her nurturing and caring to become all God made him to be. She was uniquely gifted to be a help mate. As time went on, men would look back and give credit for their success to the women who stood with them advising, nurturing, comforting and challenging.

While man and woman were created equally, they were given separate roles. They were created with a different purpose in mind. Men would be the spiritual leaders, women would be their helpers. As each person exercised these roles, the kingdom of God would advance.

The conclusion Paul makes in verse 10 is this: Because God has given the role of spiritual leadership to man and created woman to be a helpmate, then the woman should have a symbol of authority on her head.

The key for Paul was that men and women exercise the role God intended from the beginning of creation. It appears that this purpose of God was being challenged in Corinth. The Tyndale Bible Dictionary has this to say about the city of Corinth:

> *The acropolis of the city, on top of the steep, high Acro-corinth, contained the temple of Aphrodite, where 1,000 female slaves were dedicated to the service of this goddess of love. This distinctive cult of Corinth was dedicated to the veneration of Aphrodite, goddess of love, beauty and fertility, who identified with the Roman Venus. Associated with such religious practices was a general moral degradation. Corinthian morals were notoriously corrupt, when when compared to pagan Rome. (Comfort, Philip W., Elwell, Walter A., Tyndale Bible Dictionary, "Corinth", Cedar Rapids: Tyndale House Publishers, Inc. 2001.)*

With the elevation of the goddess of love and the immoral role of the many female temple servants of Aphrodite, it was important for Paul to challenge the church of Corinth to return to the God-ordained principles established in the Garden of Eden.

Paul's teaching in 1 Corinthians 11 is theological in nature. In these verses, he calls the church of Corinth to return to the purpose of God from the time of creation. He teaches that God created men and women with different roles. Despite the cultural challenges of Corinth, he encourages

women to be submissive to the purpose of God and to resist the pagan cultural influences of the day.

So far, I have not entered a discussion on the matter of
whether women should wear a veil or head covering when
praying or prophesying in the church. There are various
opinions on this in the church of our day. We can see
clearly from Paul's teaching in 1 Corinthians 11 that, if a
woman wears a veil, she is following the custom and tradition of the early church.

The question we need to ask, is whether what Paul
teaches in 1 Corinthians 11 is a command for all cultures
and times or for the church and culture of his day. Let me
conclude with a few comments on this.

First, notice that Paul begins this passage in 1 Corinthians
11:2 by commending the Corinthians for the fact that they
had maintained the traditions as he had delivered them.
This sets the tone for the rest of the passage. Paul is
speaking about traditions. As we have seen, the New Testament distinguishes "traditions" from the "commands" of
God. In 1 Corinthians 11 we have a combination of traditions and commands. The commands come in the theological teaching of Paul about the purpose for men and
women from creation. The tradition comes in how women
dressed and what was understood by their dress. For example, no woman at that time would venture outside her
home without first covering her head but they would come
to church and uncover themselves. This was shocking,
culturally inappropriate and distracting for those who worshipped.

Second, notice what Paul has to say in 1 Corinthians 11:6:

6 For if a wife will not cover her head, then she should cut her hair short. But since it is disgraceful for a wife to cut off her hair or shave her head, let her cover her head. (1 Corinthians 11)

Notice what Paul is saying here. If a woman did not cover her head, she was to cut her hair short. That would not be an issue for women of our day. Almost all the older women I know in my culture have chosen to cut their hair above their shoulder or shorter. This is not considered a shame for them in my culture. Paul's argument here would not make sense in our culture. It must be understood in the context of that day. For any women to cut her hair in that day was a shame. There is a cultural shift that has taken place. Hair styles have changed over the years.

Another cultural change has taken place over the years in Christian culture. Christian women do not always wear a head covering when outside of their home. There is no sense of shame in seeing a woman without a head-covering walking down the street in Christian cultures around the world.

The question we are left with here is this: while the commands of God never change, can Christian tradition change? The church, for example has the tradition of celebrating Easter and Christmas even though there is no command in Scripture to celebrate these two events. Queen Esther established the yearly celebration of Purim, but this was never commanded by God in the Law of Moses. Is it a sin not to celebrate one of these events? While we are bound to follow the commands of God, our traditions and cultural understanding may change. Wearing a veil outside of the home was expected of women in that day. At creation, however, Eve did not express submission to Adam by wearing a veil –in fact, they wore nothing at all. Her submission had to be expressed in a different way.

In 1 Corinthian 11 Paul speaks about the wife wearing a symbol of authority. In the culture of Corinth that symbol was a head-covering. Listen, however, to what Peter has to say to wives of his day:

1 Likewise, wives, be subject to your own husbands, so that even if some do not obey the word, they may be won without a word by the conduct of their wives, 2 when they see your respectful and pure conduct. 3 Do not let your adorning be external—the braiding of hair and the putting on of gold jewelry, or the clothing you wear— 4 but let your adorning be the hidden person of the heart with the imperishable beauty of a gentle and quiet spirit, which in God's sight is very precious. 5 For this is how the holy women who hoped in God used to adorn themselves, by submitting to their own husbands, 6 as Sarah obeyed Abraham, calling him lord. And you are her children, if you do good and do not fear anything that is frightening.
(1 Peter 3)

Like Paul, Peter challenges women to be subject to their husbands as head of the home. He reminded these women that they were not to be focused on adoring their heads and putting on jewellery but rather on putting on a gentle and quiet spirit. This, Peter told them, is what Sarah did as a sign of her submission to her husband Abraham.

Should a woman wear a veil? Maybe this depends on their culture or tradition. Remember, however, that a veil without the sign of a quiet and gentle spirit is of no value. It was this spirit that Sarah put on her head as her sign of authority.

For Consideration:

What is the difference between a tradition and a command? Can a tradition change?

What was the cultural understanding of a woman wearing a veil? When was the veil used by women? Why would it have been shocking for a woman to remove these veils in church?

What was it like to live in Corinth in the days of Paul? What was the pagan religion of the day like? How were woman in this pagan system seen and treated?

Paul challenged women of the day to go against the cultural norm and to follow instead the teaching of Scripture? How did this elevate the position of woman considering how they were treated in the pagan religion of Corinth?

Paul taught that women were to be helpers to men as they sought to lead in the church. He bases his arguments on the book of Genesis and the purpose of God in creation. What was God's purpose for men and women at creation?

Should women wear veils today? What does Peter say is the true sign of authority for a woman?

For Prayer:

Ask the Lord to help you to respect those who have a different opinion than you in this matter of women wearing head-coverings in church.

Thank the Lord for the various roles He has established in the church. Ask Him to help you to accept His purpose.

Thank the Lord that while He has roles for us to play, both women and men are important in the purpose of God for this world.

CHAPTER 6 -
THE TEACHING OF PAUL
IN 1 CORINTHIANS 14

It falls to us now to examine the teaching of Paul in 1 Corinthians 14:34-35. The context of these verses shows us that Paul was speaking to the Corinthians about their public worship services.

26 What then, brothers? When you come together, each one has a hymn, a lesson, a revelation, a tongue, or an interpretation. Let all things be done for building up. (1 Corinthians 14)

Verse 26 gives us a glimpse into a worship service in the early church. People came to worship with something to share— "each one has a hymn, a lesson, a revelation, a tongue, or an interpretation." There was an informality to this type of service. People would share as God put things on their heart. Paul has no issue with the informality of the service but does encourage the believers to share with the goal of building each other up in the faith.

The apostle also reminded the Corinthian believers that God expected order and respect in their worship service. "God is not a God of confusion but of peace", he told them in verse 36. This may indicate that the worship services of Corinth were getting a bit chaotic and confusing. It was not in the interest of the church to continue in this confusion, so Paul wrote to give some guidelines in proper worship.

We saw from verse 26 that the worship services in Corinth had various elements:

1) Singing hymns
2) A lesson or teaching
3) Revelation –prophetic in nature
4) Tongues and interpretations

There does not appear to be any order in which these events took place, but it was generally expected that the church worship service would include the above elements.

Concerning the speaking of tongues in the worship service, Paul gave this guideline to the Corinthian church:

27 If any speak in a tongue, let there be only two or at most three, and each in turn, and let someone interpret. 28 But if there is no one to interpret, let each of them keep silent in church and speak to himself and to God. (1 Corinthians 14)

It was permissible for believers to speak in tongues in the Corinthian church, but they were to remember that everything was to be done for the strengthening of the body. For this to happen, those speaking in tongues were to do so out loud, one at a time, and have an interpreter give the meaning of their words. If there was no interpreter, they were to be silent. Instead, they were to speak in tongues quietly to themselves and God (see verse 28). To allow for the use of other gifts in the worship service, the Corinthians were to only allow two or three people to speak publicly in tongues in a given worship service.

Concerning the gift of prophecy, the apostle said the following:

> *29 Let two or three prophets speak, and let the others weigh what is said. 30 If a revelation is made to another sitting there, let the first be silent. 31 For you can all prophesy one by one, so that all may learn and all be encouraged, 32 and the spirits of prophets are subject to prophets. (1 Corinthians 14)*

As with those speaking in tongues, the number of people allowed to prophesy was to be limited to two or three in a worship service. As the person with the word from the Lord spoke, other believers were to carefully weigh what was being said. The word spoken by any individual needed to be confirmed and interpreted by the larger body. Paul told the Corinthians that if a second person received a word from the Lord, the first person was to sit down and be silent. In other words, only one person was to be prophesying at a time and everyone was to be listening so that they could learn and be encouraged (verse 31).

Paul's advice to the Corinthian church may give us a hint as to what the worship services in Corinth had become. This is what I imagine. People coming to worship in the church in Corinth seemed to be isolated from each other. In one corner an individual spoke out in a tongue. In the middle of the group, another shared a word of prophecy at the same time. Behind him an individual began to sing a hymn. In another corner someone had an interpretation of the tongue spoken by the first individual. As one listened to the interpretation, another person started speaking a prophetic word. There did not seem to be any order to what was going on. Paul felt compelled to help them deal with this confusion.

It is in this context that Paul told the church that women were to remain silent.

34 the women should keep silent in the churches. For they are not permitted to speak, but should be in submission, as the Law also says. (1 Corinthians 14)

To be fair, women were not the only ones Paul said were to keep silent. He told those speaking in tongues that if there was no one to interpret their tongue they were to keep silent:

28 But if there is no one to interpret, let each of them keep silent in church and speak to himself and to God. (1 Corinthians 14)

He told the those who had a prophecy that if someone else received a word from the Lord they were to be silent:

30 If a revelation is made to another sitting there, let the first be silent. (1 Corinthians 14)

The general rule Paul gave to all the church was that if someone else was speaking, then the others were to be silent and listen.

As we examine Paul's advice in 1 Corinthians 14 about women, the question we need to ask is whether verse 34 is Paul's response to the problem of disorderly worship in Corinth only or a general principle for all churches.

To answer this, notice first Paul's use of the word "churches":

34 the women should keep silent in the churches (1 Co-rinthians 14)

Many translations include the phrase "As in all the congre-gations of the saints" (from verse 33) with the first part of verse 34 so that it reads: "As in all the congregations of the saints, the women should keep silent in the churches." Paul's use of the plural "churches" in verse 34 seems to indicate that he is not speaking about a problem in Corinth only but a general principle that the church of God was to maintain.

The second important point we need to make from verse 34 is found in the second half of the verse which says:

34 ...For they are not permitted to speak, but should be in submission, as the Law also says. (1 Corinthians 14)

Paul told the Corinthian believers that the reason a woman was not to speak but to be silent in church had to do with what the Law said about her being in submission. Paul does not quote the specific law, but the general under-standing was that the husband was the head of the wife and that as firstborn, man was the earthly spiritual head of the church (see Genesis 3:16; 1 Corinthians 11:8-10). From Paul's perspective, his teaching about the silence of women in churches applied to all churches and was based on the law of God.

The apostle goes even further in verse 35 to tell the church of Corinth that if a woman wanted to learn, she was to question her husband when they returned home.

35 If there is anything they desire to learn, let them ask
their husbands at home. For it is shameful for a woman to
speak in church (1 Corinthians 14)

Notice in verse 35 that Paul does not diminish the capacity of the woman to learn. The fact that women were present in the assembly is an indication that they were there to learn from the lesson being taught. Paul encouraged women to discuss spiritual matters with their husband in the privacy of their home.

What is the apostle saying in this passage? Do we take these statements of Paul at face value and advocate total silence for women in worship? To say that Paul is advocating absolute silence for women in church is a problem. We have seen how women in the Old Testament were permitted to sing along with men in worship (see Exodus 15:20-21; 1 Samuel 18:6-7; 2 Chronicles 35:25). They are also seen in public confession of sin (Nehemiah 8:9; Ezra 10:1). Hannah went into the temple to pray (1 Samuel 1,2). The prophetess Anna was in the temple speaking about the young child Jesus to all who looked forward to the redemption of Jerusalem (see Luke 2.38). Jesus encouraged the questions of the Samaritan woman in John 4. In the New Testament church women prayed openly with men (Acts 1:13-14). In 1 Corinthians 11 Paul advised women on how they were to cover their head while praying and prophesying in the church. For Paul to advocate total silence on the part of women in worship would go against his own personal teaching and the teaching of the rest of Scripture.

To understand what Paul is saying here, there are several key principles we need to understand. Our interpretation of his words, must be examined through these lenses.

First, verses 33 and 34 lead us to understand that Paul is teaching a universal principle for all churches:

33 ...As in all the churches of the saints, 34 the women should keep silent in the churches... (1 Corinthians 14)

Paul's instruction in these verses are not only for the church in Corinth with its unique problems but for all Christian churches.

Second, Paul's position, though there are some cultural aspects to it, is not uniquely cultural but theological in nature.

34 ...For they are not permitted to speak, but should be in submission, as the Law also says. (1 Corinthians 14)

The phrase, "as the Law also says," is the basis for his arguments. This moves the statements of Paul from being a cultural matter to a theological principle. If the discussion of Paul is purely cultural, we might be able to say that it only applied to the women of the church in Corinth. Because Paul states that his position is based on the Law, however, this moves his teaching from a localized problem to a general teaching applicable to all churches.

Third, we need to interpret what Paul is teaching here considering the rest of his teaching and the teaching of Scripture in its entirety. Scripture is the best commentary on Scripture. We have already seen that Paul had no problem with the prayers and prophecies of women in worship. Both the New Testament and the Old Testament are filled with women speaking in public religious celebrations.

Fourth, 1 Corinthians 14 must also be interpreted in its immediate and cultural context. Let me explain.

The worship service of the Corinthian church consisted of singing, a lesson from Scripture, prophetic revelations, and tongues. (see 1 Corinthians 14:26). There was a significant amount of interaction in these services. For example, a person who spoke in a tongue was to be interpreted by another person (1 Corinthians 14:27). If a person had a prophetic revelation, those present were to "weigh" what was said (1 Corinthians 14:29). Commenting on the teaching that took place in the synagogue Adam Clarke said this:

It was permitted to any man to ask questions, to object, altercate, attempt to refute, etc. in the synagogue; but this liberty was not allowed to any woman. (Clarke, Adam, Commentary on the Bible by Adam Clarke (1831), 1 Corinthians 14:34, Marion, Iowa: Laridian, Inc. 2015)

It appears from this that even the preaching and teaching of the early church was interactive with questions and discussion. We have an example of this in Luke 2. On this occasion the Lord Jesus was just a boy. His parents were returning home, but Jesus stayed with the teachers at the temple. Supposing Him to be with friends, his parents did not notice his absence for some time. When they discovered His absence, they returned to the temple to find Him. Notice where they found Him and what He was doing:

46 After three days they found him in the temple, sitting among the teachers, listening to them and asking them questions. 47 And all who heard him were amazed at his understanding and his answers. (Luke 2)

We have another example of this interactive style of teaching in Matthew 21:

23 And when he entered the temple, the chief priests and the elders of the people came up to him as he was teaching, and said, "By what authority are you doing these things, and who gave you this authority?" 24 Jesus answered them, "I also will ask you one question, and if you tell me the answer, then I also will tell you by what authority I do these things. 25 The baptism of John, from where did it come? From heaven or from man?" And they discussed it among themselves, saying, "If we say, 'From heaven,' he will say to us, 'Why then did you not believe him?' 26 But if we say, 'From man,' we are afraid of the crowd, for they all hold that John was a prophet." 27 So they answered Jesus, "We do not know." And he said to them, "Neither will I tell you by what authority I do these things. (Matthew 21)

We see from these verses the freedom the men had to interrupt the teaching of Jesus with questions and challenges. This was likely the format used in the early church. Tongues were interpreted, prophesies were weighed and discussed, the Scripture lesson was questioned and debated.

In 1 Corinthians 14:35 Paul told the women to be silent and if they wanted to learn more they were to ask their husbands at home:

35 If there is anything they desire to learn, let them ask their husbands at home. For it is shameful for a woman to speak in church. (1 Corinthians 14)

This seems to give the context for the silence Paul is requiring. The silence of women is connected here to the time of learning or to the preaching and discussion of the word. Men were given the responsibility to teach the lesson. Other men debated and challenged the teacher on what he was saying. It appears that Paul is telling the women to be silent and listen during this discussion and debate. A woman publicly challenging the teaching of the church leader was not seen as submissive.

This is not to say that the women would not have questions about what was being taught. She may have some important correction or addition that needed to be made in the instruction she heard. She was encouraged, however, not to publicly challenge her spiritual leader but to discuss the matter with her husband at home. If she had a legitimate point to make, he could take it to the leader and discuss it with him. She was to go through the proper channels and respect the leadership God ordained.

The input of women was valuable in the early church. They were, however, to be in submission to the leadership God had ordained from creation. Women who had issues to discuss with their leadership were encouraged not to do so in public meetings but discuss the matter with their husband and together they could take the appropriate steps. Paul's concern in this section of Scripture is for order in the worship service and respect for the God-ordained leadership of the church.

For Consideration:

What do we learn about the form of worship in the church in Corinth? How does your church worship style differ from the form used in Corinth?

The worship services of the early church seemed to be quite interactive in nature with discussions and debate.

What are the strengths of this style of worship? What are the weakness of this style of worship?

How important is order in the worship service?

Paul teaches some important principles here in these verses. How do we know that what the apostle teaches here is not only for the local Corinthian church at the time but for all churches?

How would the silence of women in the debates be a sign of respect and submission?

Does Paul discourage the intellectual participation of women in the church? Give some examples of how women in the early church were encouraged to learn and grow.

For Prayer:

Thank the Lord for the different ways we can worship Him and grow in our Christian faith.

Ask the Lord to give you wisdom to know if your church worship style is encouraging and blessing those who attend.

Ask the Lord to help you to respect those to whom He has given authority in the church. Ask God to forgive you for times you may have spoken wrongly of them our challenged their authority.

Ask the Lord to help you to know the right channels to go through to address your concerns for your church and its teaching so that you are respecting His purpose and the leadership He has ordained.

CHAPTER 7 -

THE TEACHING OF PAUL

IN 1 TIMOTHY 2

We come now to the final passage we will consider on Paul's teaching about the role of women in the church. Writing to Timothy, the apostle said:

8 I desire then that in every place the men should pray, lifting holy hands without anger or quarrelling; 9 likewise also that women should adorn themselves in respectable apparel, with modesty and self-control, not with braided hair and gold or pearls or costly attire, 10 but with what is proper for women who profess godliness—with good works. 11 Let a woman learn quietly with all submissiveness. 12 I do not permit a woman to teach or to exercise authority over a man; rather, she is to remain quiet. 13 For Adam was formed first, then Eve; 14 and Adam was not deceived, but the woman was deceived and became a transgressor. 15 Yet she will be saved through childbearing—if they continue in faith and love and holiness, with self-control. (1 Timothy 2)

The apostle begins by exhorting men to pray, lifting holy hands without anger or quarrelling. It is important that we understand the cultural context of these verses. In the previous chapter we examined the worship services in Corinth. These services appeared to be quite interactive and involved speaking in tongues and the interpreting of those tongues, words of prophecy and a judging of the prophetic word, instruction in the Scriptures and discussion of the passage under consideration. In the Jewish synagogue, these discussions could become quite heated, leading to quarrelling and anger. We have examples of this in the reaction of the religious leaders to the teaching of Jesus in the temple. Sometimes they came out of the temple wanting to kill Jesus.

Consider, for example, two encounters of Jesus and the chief priests as recorded in Matthew 21:

14 And the blind and the lame came to him in the temple, and he healed them. 15 But when the chief priests and the scribes saw the wonderful things that he did, and the children crying out in the temple, "Hosanna to the Son of David!" they were indignant, 16 and they said to him, "Do you hear what these are saying?" And Jesus said to them, "Yes; have you never read,
"'Out of the mouth of infants and nursing babies you have prepared praise'?"
17 And leaving them, he went out of the city to Bethany and lodged there. (Matthew 21)

Notice that the chief priests and scribes interrupted Jesus and challenged His ministry in the temple. They were angry (see verse 15) with Jesus and what He was doing. This ultimately led to Jesus leaving the temple.

Consider another encounter between Jesus and the chief priest in the temple. This time Jesus was teaching those who had gathered to listen.

23 And when he entered the temple, the chief priests and the elders of the people came up to him as he was teaching, and said, "By what authority are you doing these things, and who gave you this authority?" 24 Jesus answered them, "I also will ask you one question, and if you tell me the answer, then I also will tell you by what authority I do these things. 25 The baptism of John, from where did it come? From heaven or from man?" And they discussed it among themselves, saying, "If we say, 'From heaven,' he will say to us, 'Why then did you not believe him?' 26 But if we say, 'From man,' we are afraid of the crowd, for they all hold that John was a prophet." 27 So they answered Jesus, "We do not know." And he said to them, "Neither will I tell you by what authority I do these things.

While it is not our purpose to discuss the content of Jesus' teaching that day, what is important for us to note is the way these chief priests were free to interrupt the teaching of Jesus and question His authority. Ultimately, the answers Jesus gave left these leaders frustrated and angry with Him.

It was from this cultural context that the early believers came. Men were free to interact, question and debate those who were teaching in the temple while others listened. There were times when disagreements could lead to angry outbursts and quarrelling. It is for this reason that Paul challenged Christian men to lift holy hands when they prayed. Holy hands were hands that were not stained with sin. In this case, they were free from anger and quarrelling.

In other words, Paul challenges men to put aside their anger and differences when they came to worship.

Paul then turned his attention to the women who gathered to pray alongside of the men. While men were to put aside their anger and pray with holy hands lifted to God, women were to be modest and self-controlled.

9 likewise also that women should adorn themselves in respectable apparel, with modesty and self-control, not with braided hair and gold or pearls or costly attire, 10 but with what is proper for women who profess godliness— with good works. (1 Timothy 2)

Paul told women to dress in respectable clothing when they came to worship. He reminded them that the worship service was not the place to make an impression with their braided hair, gold, pearls and expensive clothes (see verse 9). Instead, women were to come before the Lord with a godly character as those who served Him faithfully. This would please the Lord more than all their fancy clothes and jewellery.

Paul goes on in verse 11 to give another guideline for women:

11 Let a woman learn quietly with all submissiveness. (1 Timothy 2)

Remember the context of verse 8. While men were permitted to challenge those who were teaching, this privilege was not given to women. Paul told Timothy that women were to learn quietly and with submissiveness. Paul went on in verse 12 to say:

12 I do not permit a woman to teach or to exercise authority over a man; rather, she is to remain quiet. (1 Timothy 2)

Paul did not permit a woman to teach or exercise authority over a man. It is important that we keep this phrase together. Paul is not saying that women cannot teach at all. In fact, there are many occasion in Scripture where women are commended for their teaching or even commanded to teach. The writer to the Proverbs commanded his readers not to forsake the teaching of their mother:

8 Hear, my son, your father's instruction,
and forsake not your mother's teaching,
9 for they are a graceful garland for your head
and pendants for your neck. (Proverbs 1)

The teaching of a mother is compared to a graceful garland for the head and a pendant for the neck. The son who walked in the teaching of a godly mother was an honourable son.

Paul commanded older women to teach younger women in Titus 2:

3 Older women likewise are to be reverent in behaviour, not slanderers or slaves to much wine. They are to teach what is good, 4 and so train the young women to love their husbands and children, 5 to be self-controlled, pure, working at home, kind, and submissive to their own husbands, that the word of God may not be reviled. (Titus 2)

Paul recognised the very important role of Timothy's mother and grandmother in teaching and passing on to him a sincere faith:

5 I am reminded of your sincere faith, a faith that dwelt first in your grandmother Lois and your mother Eunice and now, I am sure, dwells in you as well. (2 Timothy 1)

When Paul said: "I do not permit a woman to teach or to exercise authority over a man," he is not speaking about any teaching but rather about a teaching that exercises authority over a man. Paul argument is not based on any difference between the intellectual ability of the sexes but rather on the fact that Adam was formed first:

13 For Adam was formed first, then Eve… (1 Timothy 2)

Notice how he begins verse 13 with the word "for." This indicates that it is the reason for his argument in verse 12. While women have the same intellectual capacity as man and are as capable as men to teach, God chose to form Adam first and ordained him to be the head and leader. As the firstborn head, it is the responsibility of man to be the chief leader and teacher in the church. This, according to Paul was what God intended from creation.

Notice, second from 1 Timothy 2:14, that Paul also based his argument on the fact that Eve was deceived but Adam was not.

14 and Adam was not deceived, but the woman was deceived and became a transgressor. (1 Timothy 2)

How can the apostle say that Adam was not deceived when he also ate the forbidden fruit? Notice that Paul called Eve a transgressor but did not apply the same accusation to Adam. The rest of Scripture, however, makes is quite clear that Adam also was a transgressor:

*7 But like Adam they transgressed the covenant;
there they dealt faithlessly with me. (Hosea 6)*

To understand what Paul is teaching here we need to understand it from the perspective of what took place in the Garden of Eden at that moment Satan tempted Eve. Genesis 3:1-7 tells the story of what happened that day. In the story, Satan had a conversation with Eve. In that conversation they debated the merits of eating from the Tree of the Knowledge of Good and Evil. While Eve understood the command of God not to eat from the tree (see Genesis 3:2), Satan's arguments were very appealing. He convinced Eve to pick a fruit from the tree and eat it.

Let's pause and consider what happened at that precise moment in time. Eve disobeyed God. This was the first sin. For the first time in the history of the earth, a human being rebelled against God. The impact of that act was enormous. It brought shame (Genesis 3:7), separation from God (Genesis 3:8), fear (Genesis 3:10), pride (Genesis 3:11-13), pain and suffering (Genesis 3:16), broken relationships (Genesis 3:16), a cursing of the earth (Genesis 3:17) and death (Genesis 3:18). In that brief moment, the disease of sin was unleashed on the earth. From that time forward, every human being ever born would be separated from God, living in a body cursed by sin. Human beings would live on this earth with the understanding that time is short, and death is certain. This was the result of what Eve did that day. At that moment of time, Eve brought the curse of sin on the earth. She would be the first transgressor. All this took place even before she brought the forbidden fruit to Adam.

Remember that Paul's discussion about Eve is in the context of his teaching that a woman was not to teach or exercise authority over a man. What is the connection between a woman not being permitted to teach and this discussion about man being created first and Eve being deceived by Satan?

Notice that there are two firsts in this verse. Man was created first and woman was deceived first. There were implications to both events. Man was created first, so he would be charged, as the firstborn with the obligation of being the spiritual head. Eve was deceived first and would be charged with a very different role:

15 Yet she will be saved through childbearing—if they continue in faith and love and holiness, with self-control.
(1 Timothy 2)

Paul reminded women that they would be saved through childbearing if they continued "in faith and love and holiness, with self-control." (1 Timothy 2). There are two ways we can understand this verse.

First, the word "saved" is not always used to speak of salvation from sin. It literally means being delivered from trouble or to be kept safe in a difficult or deadly situation. It is possible that Paul is telling women that while they would experience pain in childbearing, the Lord would keep them through this pain and bless them with children. They were not to take this grace of God for granted. In gratitude to God women were to walk in faith, love, holiness and self-control.

There is, however, a second and more important interpretation we must consider. In this interpretation we understand the word "saved" to refer to salvation from sin and the curse of sin. Paul is telling women that by means of this natural, God-given process of child bearing, the salvation of God's people would be accomplished. One day an angel appeared to a young woman named Mary and told her that she would conceive and bear a son. She was to name that son, Jesus, because He would save His people from their sin (Luke 1:26-33; Matthew 1:21). Through pain and suffering Mary would give birth to her son. This son would release His people from the effects of the fall. Sin came to the earth when the woman Eve opened the door in the Garden of Eden. Salvation, however, would also come through the fruit of her womb.

What is Paul saying? He is saying that God has a purpose. That purpose includes both men and women, but their roles are different. Because men were created first they were to be spiritual leaders in their church and family. Woman, was not to take on that role, instead, God had another role for her. She would be the bearer of the child who would bring salvation to the ends of the earth.

In 1 Timothy 2, Paul challenges women to be learn quietly and in submission because Adam was created first and charged by God to be the leader of his home and church. She was to allow him to exercise that role and submit to his leadership. He also reminds women that while they were not charged by God to be spiritual leaders in the church they had a vital role to play as well. They were to bring the salvation of God to this earth by means of the children they bore. As each child was born, he or she formed a chain the lead up to the birth of the Lord Jesus and the salvation he offers. As each child is born after Christ, the kingdom of God is expanded, and the return of the Lord draws nearer. When that last child, according to God's purpose is born, then the Lord will return, and the salvation of His people will be complete. Paul challenges men and women to accept the role God has given them from the very beginning of time.

Paul theology of the role of men and women in the church is linked strongly to the creation purpose of God. The fact that Paul forbids women to teach or take authority over a man has nothing to do with their ability but everything to do with the purpose of God. The issue here for us is not whether a woman can lead as well as a man but whether we are ready to accept what God wants and how He wants to advance His kingdom.

For Consideration:

What do we learn about the early church and the freedom there was to debate and challenge those who were teaching?

At what point does questioning and debating a teacher become a challenge to the authority of that teacher?

Does Paul command absolute silence for women in worship services? What were women permitted to do in the presence of men in worship?

What is the theological basis for Paul's position on women not teaching or having authority over a man?

Paul encouraged women to dress modestly as they came to worship. How would you define modest? Why is the worship service not the place for women to dress to impress?

Does Scripture forbid a woman to teach at all? In what circumstances did the apostle encourage women to teach?

What was the impact of Eve opening the door to sin? How did God use women to bring the solution to the problem of sin?

For Prayer:

Thank the Lord that while sin has devastated this earth, the Lord Jesus was born of a woman to bring salvation.

Ask the Lord to help you to show respect for those He has ordained to teach you His ways. Thank the Lord for the gifts and calling He has placed on the lives of these individuals.

Ask the Lord to help you to walk in submission to His purpose for the church. Ask Him to show you if you have been rebelling against that purpose in any way.

CHAPTER 8 -
PRINCIPLES FOR
APPLICATION

Over the last seven chapters we have examined the teaching of Scripture on the distinct roles of men and women in ministry. I trust that I have been faithful in my interpretation and examination of the passages that speak to this issue. I have no doubt, however, that this book has stirred up many questions about how to apply these passages in the life of the church. Not all believers will apply these truths in the same way. In this concluding chapter let me leave you with some key Biblical principles to guide your thinking and application of the truths we have studied.

Authority of the Word of God in Faith and Life

As believers in the Lord Jesus, we are committed to the truth of Scripture. The Bible is our guide in all matters that concern our faith and life practices. There are times when we may not like what the Bible is saying. We may not understand the reasoning behind the principles it teaches but we are bound as believers to walk in its teaching. God has

laid out His purposes for the church in the pages of Scripture. This must be our guide.

The Bible is an Unchanging Truth for Today

Not only must we as believers accept the Bible as God's
authoritative Word, but we must also see it as His truth for
today. The truth of the Scriptures, as it was taught by the
apostles, was not just for the believers of their day but also
for us. The truth of Scripture does not change with the
times. I understand that we are living in a different culture
than those of the New Testament period, but the principles
God teaches in His Word are for all cultures and all times.

I have heard too many people dismiss whole sections of
Scripture saying that they no longer apply to them today. I
have seen too may Christians base their theology on culture and not on the truth of Scripture. Their understanding
of what is acceptable practice is not based on the teaching
of Scripture but on what is accepted in their society. God's
truth does not change with culture. It remains steady and
unchanging. It confronts our society and culture.

If we cannot agree on these two principles, then the re-
mainder of this chapter will not make any sense to you. My
purpose in this study has been to discover what the Bible
has to say about the distinct roles of women and men in
ministry. I believe that what the Bible teaches is God's purpose for the church today. Having said this, let me leave
you with a few insights and principles that may help in ap-
plying the truth we have discussed in this study.

God's Purpose from Creation

As we examined the account of creation in Genesis 1-3 we discovered that God had a specific purpose in mind when He created man and woman. Both were created in the image of God (Genesis 1:27). Both were given dominion over the creatures of the earth (Genesis 1:28). Man and woman, however, were not created in the same way. Man was created from the dust of the ground (Genesis 2:7). Woman was created from man (Genesis 2:21-22). Woman was created by God to be a helper for man (Genesis 2:18). As the firstborn, man was to be head of his family and provide the leadership it needed.

This creation principle is the basis for the New Testament position on the differing roles of men and women in church life (see 1 Corinthians 11:8, 9; 1 Timothy 2:13,14). In the decisions we make about the roles of men and women in the church, we should ask the following question: Are we walking in harmony with the creation purpose of God for men and women?

Freedom for Women to Minister in Biblical Ways

Another important principle we need to maintain has to do with the freedom the Scriptures give to women to minister. I have been in churches that have hindered women to ministry in Biblical ways. As we examine the many examples of Scripture we see women involved in many various aspects of ministry. They worshipped in the presence of men (1 Samuel 18:6-7). They sat with under the teaching of the Word of God (Nehemiah 8:1-3). They even exhorted men to take on their role as leaders (Judges 4:6-9). Women worked at the entrance to the temple (1 Samuel 2:22). They were used by God to bring great deliverance for His people (Judges 4; Judges 9:50-55; 1 Samuel 25). Women were commended for their assistance and support of the apostles (Philippians 4:2-3). Older women were commanded to teach younger women (Titus 2:3-5). They prophesied in the church (1 Corinthians 11:3-5).

What is important for us to see here is that the Bible does not restrain women or keep them from ministering. There is great freedom in Scripture for women to minister and serve the Lord under the authority he has ordained. Are we giving women in our churches the freedom Scripture gives to serve the Lord and to use their spiritual gifts?

The Authority God has Ordained

As we examined the teaching of the apostle Paul, it is quite clear that he taught that man was the head of his family and church (see 1 Corinthians 11:3). Paul bases this theology on the creation purpose of God for man and woman. The apostle Paul challenges women to be in submission to that leadership. They are to do this, not because they are inferior or less capable but because this is the purpose of God.

The principle of submission to spiritual leadership that God has ordained does not just apply to women. I have been in churches where men in the congregation felt the need to challenge its leadership, refusing to submit to the discipline or the counsel of its leaders. These men need to understand that God has ordained His leadership in the church and expects them to respect its authority (see Romans 13:1-7). We need to beware of those who serve (whether they be male or female), who show no regard for the authority God has ordained in the church.

Authority in the Bible

Paul told women that they were not to exercise authority over a man (1 Timothy 2:12). This is easy enough to understand on the surface but how does it work itself out in the life of the church? What constitutes a position of authority? In many churches, for example, men alone are permitted to take up the church offering. Is taking up the church offering exercising authority over a man or simply an act of service?

If we are to understand what Paul is saying about a woman not exercising authority over a man, we need to understand how God expects men to exercise authority in the church. An examination of Scripture seems to show that the Lord expected men to exercise their authority in two specific ways.

The first way men were to exercise authority was in the general oversight of spiritual and family life. God chose men to be leaders of the tribes of Israel. He chose male priests to oversee the spiritual lives of His people in Israel. Jesus chose male disciples to follow Him and establish the church as spiritual leaders. The apostles chose male deacons and elders to be spiritual heads of the churches they established. As spiritual heads of their family, husbands and fathers could overrule vows made by a wife or daughter (see Numbers 30:6-8). These men were accountable to God for the spiritual and general well-being of their family and nation.

The second way men were to exercise authority was in teaching and preaching the Word of God. In 1 Corinthians 14:34-35 Paul commanded women to be silent in the church and if they had any questions they were to ask their husband at home. In 1 Timothy 2:11-12 the apostle told

Timothy that he did not permit a woman to teach or to exercise authority over a man but instead she was to be quiet and learn in submission. Notice the connection in these passages between teaching and submission to authority.

We do not always see a connection between teaching and authority. This authority, however, comes from two factors. First, from the fact that the subject of the teaching is the authoritative and holy Word of God and second from the fact that those who are teaching have been called of God to do so. These teachers are God's representatives, chosen to reveal His purpose through His authoritative Word. This position carries with it the authority of God. It is a position that is to be respected. From my understanding of Scripture, God has chosen men to carry this responsibility as spiritual leaders of His people. As we seek to understand the role of women in the church, we should ask ourselves if the roles they are exercising relieve men of their God-given responsibility to give oversight and teaching in the body.

If There is No Man

When my wife and I first went to the mission field, we were sent to a church that had been planted by two women from England. They had come to the country to teach children in the school system. As they taught and shared about Jesus, many of these children became Christians. The ladies felt the call of God to share the gospel with the families of these children The result was that parents of these children began to come to the Lord. The next step was to disciple these families and to gather them together in worship. They began to meet on Sundays and the two English women taught and preached the Word of God each week.

This was the beginning of the Christian church in that country.

I have shared this story with people throughout the years. Some that I have shared this story with felt that it was wrong for these women to teach and preach to these newly converted men. They felt that, as women, they should have refrained from preaching and pray instead that God would send a man to preach to these new converts. Remember, however, that there were no mature Christian men in the country who could have taken on this role. Should these women have refused to teach and disciple these men in this case? Ultimately what happened was that as these men matured in their faith and understanding of the gospel, the leadership of the church was handed over to them. Did these ladies exercise authority over these men by teaching them a truth they had never heard? I leave this for the reader to decide. We are reminded, however, of Moses' wife Zipporah, who circumcised her son, and saved the live of Moses when he had neglected his responsibilities (Exodus 4:24-26). We also recall Deborah, who led Barak into battle because he did not have the courage to go by himself (Judges 4:6-9).

A legalistic interpretation of Scripture allows for no exceptions. Those who seek to understand the spirit behind what God is teaching will work toward this goal understanding that there are times when getting there will take time and not always follow a straight path. Jesus often condemned the religious leaders of his day for their legalistic interpretation of Scripture which showed no compassion.

[23] "Woe to you, scribes and Pharisees, hypocrites! For you tithe mint and dill and cumin, and have neglected the weightier matters of the law: justice and mercy and faithfulness. These you ought to have done, without

*neglecting the others. [24] You blind guides, straining out
a gnat and swallowing a camel! (Matthew 23)*

Speaking to the Pharisees who challenged Him because
he healed a woman on the Sabbath, Jesus said:

*[15] Then the Lord answered him, "You hypocrites! Does
not each of you on the Sabbath untie his ox or his donkey
from the manger and lead it away to water it? [16] And
ought not this woman, a daughter of Abraham whom Satan bound for eighteen years, be loosed from this bond
on the Sabbath day?" (Luke
13)*

When the Pharisees came to Jesus in Mark 10 to ask his
opinion about divorce, they reminded him that Moses permitted divorce in the law. Jesus responded to them by saying:

*[5] And Jesus said to them, "Because of your hardness of
heart he wrote you this commandment. [6] But from the
beginning of creation, 'God made them male and female.'
[7] 'Therefore a man shall leave his father and mother
and hold fast to his wife, [8] and the two shall become
one flesh.' So they are no longer two but one flesh. (Mark
10)*

Jesus reminded the Pharisees that while it was always the
intention of God that when a couple married they would
become one and remain together for life, Moses permitted
divorce because of the hardness of heart. In other words,
there were extreme situations in this sinful life where the
very safety of a wife was in danger. The compassionate
thing to do was to allow a separation for the protection of
both parties, even if this was not the original intention of
God.

Why am I mentioning these passages in this context? I do so because I believe that the two English ladies who arrived from England to share the message of salvation did the compassionate thing in teaching these new male converts about Christ and developing leaders who could move the church forward.

Jesus and Moses show us that there is flexibility in the law. Compassion and mercy may at times outweigh an unbending legalistic interpretation. This does not mean we can ignore the Word of God. We should always be striving toward the purpose of God for His church but the path to get there may be confusing at times. There are many times when I have had to work in a less than perfect situation. I am far from perfect, yet God uses me as I am. He continues to change me, but I expect that this process will take the rest of my earthly life. The disciples Jesus chose were not perfect. Judas would betray Jesus. Peter would deny him. Jesus worked with them in their imperfections. I say this because not everything in life will fall in line with how we see Scripture. We will have to work with imperfection until we enter the presence of God. The older I get the more I come to understand that not everything in this sinful world is black and white. There are decisions I need to make, people I need to work with and situations I must accept that are not ideal. In these times I need to learn to fall on the side of compassion and mercy.

Dealing with Those Who Don't Agree

Let me conclude with one more point. While I have tried to explain to the best of my ability what I see the Scripture teaches on this matter of the roles of men and women in ministry, not everyone will agree with my position. They will not interpret the teaching of Paul the way I have explained it here. I remember speaking with an ordained woman pastor some years ago and asked her why she chose to follow this path. Her response was that she felt a deep call of God on her life. I did not enter a theological debate with her in this issue. I knew she was a believer and I had to leave this matter to her and God.

I have been blessed by many women in my life. One female seminary teacher brought me great personal encouragement. Of all my teachers, she is the one I remember most. The prayers and counselling of another ordained woman pastor helped me overcome some deep hurdles in my life. I am thankful to these women.

How am I to respond to genuine believers who do not interpret the Scriptures as I have in this study? Consider the example of Jesus as He spoke with the Samaritan women in John 4. The discussion between the two became quite intense. The Samaritan women challenged Jesus as a man on His theology, emphasising the difference between the Jews and the Samaritans. Even the disciples were somewhat perplexed that Jesus had entered such a debate with a Samaritan woman. Even though she openly challenged Him, Jesus did not take offense. Instead, he bore patiently with her until she came to see Him as the Messiah who had been prophesied.

Jesus demonstrated compassion for the Samaritan women, who, not only openly challenged Him as a man, but was also guilty of living a sinful life. The Lord challenges us to pray for our enemies and love those who hurt us (see Matthew 5:43-46). If this is the attitude we need to demonstrate toward our enemies, how much more should we demonstrate this same attitude to sincere believers who differ from us?

I do not have to agree with a person to pray for them. I do not have to see eye to eye in every matter to accept them as fellow believers. At the same time, however, I need to be true to my convictions and stand firm on what I see in Scripture. Walking the thin line between standing firm on my convictions and maintaining fellowship with sincere believers who differ from us is not always easy. May God help us to find the balance between holding fast to our theological position and demonstrating the love and compassion of Christ toward those who differ from us.

For Consideration:

Does the truth of Scripture change with culture and time?

How did God create man and woman? Did He have a different purpose for them at the time of creation?

Has your church restricted the role of women in ministry? If so, in what way? What more could women be Biblically involved in, in the ministry of your church?

Have women in your church taken on the role of men? Explain.

What authority has God given men? How is this authority to be exercised?

How have you treated those who disagree with you theologically? Has your attitude been a godly one?

For Prayer:

Thank the Lord that He has given us a guide in the pages of His Word for all things related to life and faith.

Ask God to help you to accept the role He has given to you as man or woman. Ask the Lord to show you if you are walking fully in His purpose.

Ask God to help you to walk respectfully with those who disagree with you. Ask Him to give you grace to love them as He loves them.

Light To My Path Book Distribution

Light To My Path (LTMP) is a book writing and distribution ministry reaching out to needy Christian workers in Asia, Latin America, and Africa. Many Christian workers in developing countries do not have the resources necessary to obtain Bible training or purchase Bible study materials for their ministries and personal encouragement. F. Wayne Mac Leod is a member of Action International Ministries and has been writing these books with a goal to distribute them to needy pastors and Christian workers around the world.

To date tens of thousands of books are being used in preaching, teaching, evangelism and encouragement of local believers in over sixty countries. Books have now been translated into a number of languages. The goal is to make them available to as many believers as possible.

The ministry of LTMP is a faith-based ministry and we trust the Lord for the resources necessary to distribute the books for the encouragement and strengthening of believers around the world. Would you pray that the Lord would open doors for the translation and further distribution of these books?

For more information about Light To My Path Book Distribution visit our website at http://ltmp-homepage.blogspot.ca

Printed in Great Britain
by Amazon